Preparation *and* Presentation

OF THE

OPERETTA

BY (Frank Ambrose]

FRANK A. BEACH

DIRECTOR OF MUSIC
AT
THE KANSAS STATE TEACHERS COLLEGE

BOSTON : Oliver Ditson Company : NEW YORK

Chicago: LYON & HEALY, INC.   London: WINTHROP ROGERS, LTD.

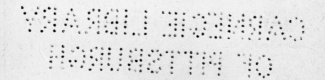

TO MY WIFE

FOREWORD

Civilization is gauged not by the way it appreciates beautiful things but by the way it produces them. Performance is vastly more important as a testimonial to beauty than is mere appreciation. This book is devoted to the task of stimulating the production of lovely music. It may be assumed that those who essay to produce music enjoy it, appreciate it, and to an extent understand it.

Frank A. Beach, the author of this book, has been a producer of lovely things in a Kansas town for more than twenty years. As the head of the music department of the Kansas State Teachers College, he has been teaching youth in this state how to make good music, how to teach others to make good music. Literally hundreds of men and women have gone forth from his department teaching his gospel to tens of thousands of children in the west. His gospel in brief is this: that to enjoy beauty one must participate in its creation, not merely stand before it in admiration. To enjoy singing one must sing. To enjoy playing one must play. Art is an active agent, not a passive force in one's life.

In this book he has taken the operetta as his theme. The operetta is one form of musical art which is easily within the compass of any neighborhood, guild or group. Mr. Beach in this book points the way to the production of this rather simple and beautiful musical art form in a technically correct and artistically delightful way.

I know of no other book which does exactly what he is trying to do: to present the stage technique understandably, to interpret the meaning of the music, and to create a whole of music, tableau, and movement which will reproduce all the joy which the composer had in his heart when he wrote the operetta.   Yet Mr. Beach has put this so plainly, and has placed it so completely at the disposal of the average school and community that this art form, the operetta, may be produced well by any painstaking, enthusiastic, intelligent group that may care to try it.

This was no easy task for Mr. Beach, however forthright and direct his instructions are.   It was a hard thing to do and he has done it well.   But chiefly this book is worth while because it teaches us to make the beauty we enjoy, to multiply our appreciation a thousand fold by performance.

W M Allen White

Emporia, Kansas, 1930

PREFACE

Since in the preface of a book a writer may hide away from the general reading public certain facts that are of interest only to the friendly cover-to-cover reader, I can perhaps best illumine the stage for my succeeding chapters by dimming, for the moment, the present and by casting on the scene the pale light of retrospection.

Years ago a little New York town was set agog by the announcement that in its Opera House, whose boards had but lately creaked to the lively steps of that too-awful-to-be-imagined musical comedy, *The Black Crook*, there was to be presented, by local talent, an opera!—Gilbert and Sullivan's *Pirates of Penzance*. As a boy-alto who had had "lessons" I was invited by the director of the opera to sing in the chorus. The thrill of those rehearsals in Mr. Shattuck's big parlor was surpassed only by the disappointment that followed the decision that it would be unwise for the Sunday School superintendent's only son to appear on the stage—even in an amateur production. But then and there this book had its beginning, for I had experienced for the first time the joy of pleasurable participation in music. It was therefore an easy matter for the manager of this same opera house, who was also an editor and traveler, to inspire me and to turn my steps toward Europe; and a few years later I found myself in the Grand Opera House in Paris—in the audience. Although assured (as what European vocal student has not been?) of an Italian debut in opera, I realized that the DeReskes were still bright in the musical firmament, and that Caruso's star was in the ascendant! Since I was already interested in solfège, I chose the virgin field of "school music."

The kaleidoscopic experience of intervening years has afforded opportunity for observing the rise and fall of theories, fads and fancies, the development of methods and material, and the shifting of emphasis from one phase of music education to another. Despite these changes, one fact stands out preeminently and unaltered, namely, that the average individual, even the student, is interested not so much in the means as in the end; today, as always, people enjoy and appreciate, in music as in other fields of activity, what they themselves do far beyond and above what is done for them. And herein lies the unusual appeal and charm of the operetta; for this combination of arts affords to a large number of people through its several avenues an opportunity for participation and self-expression.

However the musician or dramatist may regard the operetta, this form has for several centuries appealed to singers and audiences alike. The objections to the operetta which are sometimes raised are based upon conditions not necessarily inherent in it. If we remove these conditions, the operetta may continue to delight the average music lover and the public.

This book is designed to give practical help to the inexperienced supervisor and amateur director who may wish to produce an operetta. Furthermore, I venture to hope that it may be of service to those whose training in the fields of operetta presentation has been in the school of experience and who may feel, with me, the need of an adequate text on the subject of operetta. The various chapters are the outgrowth of a college course, "The Technique of Opera," which I have given and developed during twenty years' work of preparing public school supervisors and directors of music. I make no pretense at completeness, having intentionally omitted much material, such as dance steps, which are an important part of children's operettas, but which should be efficiently cared for by the physical training department, and a bibliography of operettas, which was begun a few years ago but is already out of date.

In addition to the practical aim of this volume, it is my hope that by tracing briefly the rise, development, and present possibility of the operetta I may give to the amateur producer of today a more dignified conception of this form of art. And furthermore, in a moment of high optimism, I dare to believe that this book, through its readers, may in some small measure help to stem the present tide of mediocre operettas. In commercial jargon, "when better operettas are written the supervisors will have demanded them."

I am glad to acknowledge the help of many whose suggestions and criticisms have aided in the preparation of this volume and to express my appreciation to the producers whose courtesy has made possible the reproduction of varied and attractive stage settings. Particularly am I grateful for the consideration and cooperation of those on the college campus with whom I have been intimately associated. Special thanks are due to Mrs. Mildred Gearhart of the department of English at the Kansas State Teachers College for valuable assistance and a critical reading of the entire manuscript. Finally, I am most deeply indebted to the members of my own household without whose patience and forebearance with the moods of a first author, this book would have been impossible.

Frank H Beach

Emporia, Kansas, 1930

ILLUSTRATIONS

ILLUSTRATIONS

CONTENTS

CHAPTER I

How the Operetta Came to Be

To find the beginnings of the form which later developed into the operetta of today, one must turn to the merry village plays of Greece. Sterling MacKinlay, in a most readable volume entitled *The Origin and Development of Light Opera*, defines the operetta as Comedy Melodrama, and makes interesting comment on the four Greek words which go to make up the term: Comedy,—*komos* and *ode: komos*, revel; *ode*, a poem—the subject of the song; Melodrama,—*melos*, melody—music to which the words of the song are sung; and *drama*, the action of the story.

If we regard light opera and the operetta—terms usually synonymous—as a fabric which has been woven like a bright-colored tapestry down through the centuries, we shall see that these four strands: drama, music, poetry, and mirth, like the threads in a loom, form the warp upon which has been woven, in varying colors, the pattern of the operetta. Although the motifs vary somewhat in different countries, they are for the most part surprisingly similar,—the influence of certain nations being distinguishable mainly by differences in pattern or by variations in shade and intensity of color. As we look at the fabric more intently, we may observe the flaming red of the early Grecian comedy, the golden ivory of the classic Greek drama, the warmer tints of the Strolling Players of Greece, and the murky, garish dyes of dissolute Roman comedy. And in succession we may trace the warm rose of Minstrelsy, the quiet pastel of the Mystery and Morality plays, the sunny yellow hue of Italian Opera Buffa, the rich colors of the Singspiel in Ger-

1

many, the variegated strands of Offenbach and the French operetta, the mellow browns and greens of the Ballad Opera in England, and finally, the sheen and the shimmer, with scattered threads of tinsel, which characterize the musical comedy, the operetta, and the light opera of the present day,—all appearing in more or less familiar yet varying designs, whether woven in Italy, France, Germany, England, or America.   Thus, in tracing the rise and development of the operetta we find that from the early village plays of Greece down to our present-day light operas and operettas, we can follow distinctly the four main threads or warp upon which the entire fabric of the operetta has been woven; and we see that although occasionally a strand has disappeared for a time and certain details of pattern or color have undergone a change as the tapestry has come from the looms of different countries, there has developed a more or less fixed form and design which has for more than a century remained comparatively unaltered.

The story of the rise and development of the operetta is most interesting, and offers marked contrasts,—from its beginnings with the grotesque Greek chorus in their goatskin costumes playing before audiences of thousands, through the period ushered in when a group of players presented Peri's *Daphne* to a select company in Bardi's palace on the Arno, down to the nineteenth century with its operas of Gilbert and Sullivan, the musical comedies of Victor Herbert, and school operettas ad infinitum.   A casual study reveals the reason for the favor with which the operetta has been received.   For, in contrast to Grand Opera, the lighter form has ever been a natural growth, often self-sown, flowering rapidly in the soil of popular appeal and bearing fruit for which no taste has had to be cultivated.   To the appeal of music and the drama, Opera Comique added the spoken dialogue, and Opera Buffa renewed that charm of humor which characterizes alike *The Barber of Seville, The Tales of Hoffman, The Chimes of Normandy,* and *The Mikado* and *Pinafore.*

It remained for a present-day composer—Humperdinck—to add a new strand to the fabric of the operetta—the spirit of childhood. Up to the middle of the present century the operetta was designed for adult performance and for adult audiences. But *Hänsel and Gretel* was written by Humperdinck for his own children; and its fairy-like subject and masterly treatment undoubtedly paved the way for worth-while operettas and other dramatic productions in which special consideration was given to children both as members of the cast and of the audience. Whereas *Hänsel and Gretel* was written for professional production, operettas of today employ amateurs—the young people of a community and the children of the public schools.

CHILDREN AND THE OPERETTA

We find the participation of children in the drama during the Greek plays, in the ceremonials of the Druids, and in the Mystery and Morality Plays of the Middle Ages. Later, children played an important part in the masks and pageants of England and in plays upon the continent. But these plays were written for adult audiences and often were ill-suited for the eyes and ears of children. In the eighteenth century, however, Mme. De Genlis established in France a theater of education for children. There, in an out-door theater, child-players themselves presented to audiences of children, plays written for children. By the middle of the nineteenth century the children's operetta had made its appearance in Great Britain and later it found its way into the United States. The first operetta for children of which we have any knowledge was based upon the experience of *Little Boy Blue, Miss Muffet,* and *Mother Goose.* It is not known whether this operetta developed after the manner of folk-plays and folk-songs, or whether it was the work of an

HÄNSEL AND GRETEL
(Perfect rhythm, posture, and costume)

unknown author. In any case, this new form of expression became a source of delight to many children of the English-speaking race.

Two conditions in the United States delayed the adoption of the operetta as a form of expression for children: the first of these was the fact that children had not learned to sing; the second, the fact that the operetta was a form of dramatic entertainment, and as such it was more or less under the ban of the church. During the closing decades of the nineteenth century, singing schools, which were open to children as well as adults, became the vogue; the church was open to these as a meeting place and a winter's series of lessons culminated in the presentation of a cantata frequently given in dramatic form. Thus the church unwittingly paved the way for amateur opera.

Meantime the éclat with which the Wagnerian Operas were received at the Metropolitan in New York City inspired the building of a "Grand Opera House" in practically every city and hamlet. These opera houses were a kind of concrete expression of the desire for what seemed unattainable, —namely, Grand Opera; for in them were held political meetings, patent medicine shows, revival services, and theatrical road productions—in short, every type of performance except opera. Suddenly, however, *Pinafore*, *The Mikado*, and other Gilbert and Sullivan operas became available to amateurs, and at last the opera house came into its own when the graduates of the singing schools hastened to join hands with the soloists of the church choir in "presenting" amateur opera.

In the meantime public school music had not only given to children a knowledge of note reading but it had also developed what is far more important—a love for and a facility in singing. The closing of each school term was therefore marked by "exhibitions"; these programs included cantatas, action songs, and tableaux. Soon operettas appeared.   These ran the gamut from *Cock Robin, The Three Bears, Seven Old Ladies of Lavender Town, Bobby Shaftoe,* to *The House That Jack Built* and *The Captain of Plymouth*—with occasional productions of *Pinafore, The Pirates of Penzance,* and *The Chimes of Normandy* presented by ambitious high schools.

The opening of the twentieth century was marked by increased interest in dramatic and operetta productions on the part of amateurs, the operetta becoming a fixed event in the annual program of the average school.   The favor with which this form of entertainment was received led to a greater demand.   The result of this demand has encouraged the publication of a constantly increasing number of operettas, varying so widely in their degrees of excellence as to challenge the judgment of the discriminating producer and to raise a doubt as to the value of the average operetta of today.

CHAPTER II

Is the Operetta Worth While

Notwithstanding the popularity of the operetta it has not been carefully evaluated in order to determine whether or not it should have a place in the field of amateur expression and in the educational programs of our schools. This lack of evaluation, together with the large number of mediocre operettas, gives rise to an important question—that is, "Is the operetta worth while?" In discussing this question we may well consider the values which accrue to those who participate and the effect of the presentation of the operetta upon the community at large. Furthermore, we should ask, "Are there tangible, usable results which justify the inclusion of the operetta in the busy life of our communities and in the crowded and complex school curriculum?"

Although in our discussion we shall consider this question frequently from the standpoint of the school, the amateur should bear in mind that the values of a good operetta are the same whether it is produced by the pupils in the school or by the adults of a community.

A MEANS OF SELF-EXPRESSION

Few instincts are more universal than an individual's desire to give outward expression to his thoughts and emotions. In the history of the race and of the individual this love of self-expression has constantly manifested itself. The make-believe play of the child, the creation of a masterpiece by the artist,—each, in its way, is an evidence of this same instinct. The operetta, through its several avenues, affords an almost ideal medium of expression, and to a larger group

7

than any other school or community project, with the exception of the pageant; it futhermore gives opportunity for the play of the imagination, for satisfying the dramatic instinct, and for musical expression. Although there may appear, side by side in the performance of an operetta, the slightly musical pupil and the singer, the timid child and the precocious young actor, there is an opportunity for all of them to give vent to some degree of self-expression.

POISE

Still another valuable asset of the operetta is the opportunity which it presents for the development of poise. Participation in the operetta enables young people to acquire a sense of ease and at-homeness in doing something before others—a confidence which amounts to a conscious poise of mind and body.

A POINT OF CONTACT

Nor should one forget, in evaluating the school operetta, how distinctly important is the point of contact which it provides between the parents and the community at large and the school. In view of the fact that comparatively few parents ever visit the class room, and that only a limited number of taxpayers take time to attend exhibits and departmental displays, a medium such as the operetta is highly valuable. Few programs seem to afford audiences as great pleasure as does the school operetta; it seems to be a lodestone which attracts many who are vitally interested in, as well as those who are remotely concerned with, what is going on in the school. The pleasure afforded to the school community; the gratification which results from seeing, even in a minor role or in a chorus part, one's own child or a neighbor's; and the varied appeals of the operetta itself,—all combine to make it a unique medium through which a school may appeal to its own particular and intimate audience.

In a similar manner the operetta, when produced by adults and young people of a community, affords an excellent point of contact between the music-loving and dramatically inclined group of amateurs and the community as a whole.

A LEISURE-TIME ACTIVITY

The complete preparation of an operetta affords a most worth-while activity for the amateurs of a community; moreover this preparation affords a splendid leisure-time activity for young people and adults alike. In connection with the school operetta an important question arises as to what relationship the preparation bears to the student's daily schedule; for the effectiveness of an operetta is in a large measure dependent upon what hours of the day are assigned for its preparation. The average operetta requires not less than twenty-five singing rehearsals and seven stage rehearsals. Although this is too great an amount of time to be taken from the after-school hours of the pupil, some of this preparation may well occupy a part of his leisure time. The far-sighted director will therefore confer with the principal and others directly concerned with the problem of distributing the time to be devoted to the rehearsals, and will then make out in advance a schedule which will be fair to all departments. In this schedule at least one-half the time required should be taken from the regular school day. The arrangement of such a program will conserve the strength of the participants, avoid conflict with scheduled and extra events, encourage cooperation, and avoid serious encroachment upon the leisure hours of the student and the director. For a pupil in school, then, a part of the preparation of an operetta may well occupy some of his leisure time; for the adult, the preparation of an operetta is a worth-while expenditure of his leisure hours.

A survey of one hundred typical cities discloses the fact that the majority of superintendents of these communities look with favor upon the operetta; although admitting that the preparation and production make heavy demands upon the supervisor, they believe that the ability to choose worthwhile material, to secure the cooperation of different departments in the school, and to carry through successfully the production of an operetta is a desirable qualification of an efficient supervisor. Many of these educators regard the operetta as a desirable type of activity because it provides a medium for valuable training to the participants; because it affords an opportunity for several groups to share in a common project, and because it makes a distinct contribution to the school and to its community.

INCENTIVE

In determining whether or not the operetta is worth while, there is another question which should be considered, namely, "Does the study of the operetta serve as a stimulus,—does it furnish an incentive for further participation in music?" Since most people do best those things which they enjoy doing, it is important that whatever form of music is given a place in the school curriculum, it should be measured by the yardstick of its value as an incentive. One needs only to consider the zest with which students enter into the production of an operetta in contrast to the all-too-frequent decrease of interest in most forms of music as they go from grades to high school to be convinced that students do need and respond to such an incentive as the operetta furnishes. The discriminating supervisor will, therefore, take advantage of this appeal of the operetta. Furthermore, he can and should make the worth-while operetta serve as a stepping-stone to an appreciation of the better material often offered in the cantata; for the supervisor who limits to

operettas alone the music material used in public performance by his vocal groups, is doing a gross injustice to his
students and to his profession. Obviously, then, the operetta
can and should justify its place in the school curriculum by
its power to serve as an incentive for further participation
in music.

A PARTNERSHIP PROJECT

Of equal importance with the foregoing advantages of the
operetta is the opportunity which it provides for cooperative
effort between the various departments of the school. For
since the operetta draws its participants from all these
departments, it should, if effectively presented, become a
partnership project. That is, it should serve as something
of a subject-leveler with which to counteract the rather
frequent tendency of some departments to stress unduly the
importance of their subjects at the expense of other subjects
in the curriculum. For, consciously or unconsciously, the
average teacher in the public schools is prone to overem-
phasize her own subject. Even music, one must admit,
might be unduly stressed, if time permitted!

Now, may not the operetta be used to counteract such a
situation—to bring to something of a level, at least for the
time being, subjects which are sometimes considered aristocratic and those which are, on the other hand, thought of as
plebeian? Indeed, we find that not infrequently it has been
the operetta which has opened the door of cooperation to
certain departments that otherwise have rarely had an opportunity to function in the life of the school. In fact the
operetta when presented as a cooperative effort may so unify
the different interests in the school or in the community, and
so make of its preparation a partnership project that its
final production becomes a high spot in the year's program.

In our consideration of the operetta, then, we have found
that it provides for the individual a useful medium for the

employment of some of his leisure time; that it supplies him an opportunity for self-expression and affords a medium through which he may develop poise; that it provides for the school a partnership project and establishes an added relationship between the parents and the activities of the school, as well as an excellent point of contact between the music amateurs and the community.   In view, then, of these tangible results which justify the time and effort required for the production, we may answer our question,—the operetta is worth while.

CHAPTER III

Amateur Opera for Adult Expression

One measure of the value of our education is the degree to which it carries over from grades to high school, and from high school to adult years. Music, particularly in its concerted forms, affords unusual opportunity for such a transmission of interest. For the pleasure derived from the presentation of the operetta and the cantata in the school years may find its counterpart in the adult life of a community through mature expression in the form of choral singing and the amateur opera. But have the adults in a community the time and inclination for the production of amateur opera? For answer may we ask: is this, primarily and exclusively, a jazz age? Can only the unusual, the bizarre, the *risqué* awaken a response? Are the adults of our communities so effete, so surfeited with effortless enjoyment that they have lost the power of initiative and become immune to the satisfaction which results from creating one's own pleasure? Have the time-saving inventions of today actually left less time for avocations? Has the physical and mental inertia inspired by the "talkies" and the radio stifled all ambition for accomplishment along cultural lines? We feel sure that the answer to these questions cannot be an unequivocal "Yes," for as there are today those people who feel the beauty of a waltz rhythm and respond to the thrill of a simple melody, so there are many who still believe that individual effort is desirable and that the entertainment which we ourselves create is the most worth while. Moreover, the adage "use or lose" may well be a stop signal alike to the physically inactive automobile driver and to that

13

individual whose powers of self-expression are about to atrophy. For those who feel this desire and need for participation there is certainly no more enjoyable and profitable form of entertainment available than that offered by amateur opera.

OPERA A VEHICLE FOR ORGANIZATIONS

As the operetta supplies a valuable medium through which students in the grades and high school may gain poise and develop freedom in self-expression, in much the same way the adults in a community may utilize amateur opera; but as a rule amateur opera serves the community best when it functions through organizations. Since the members in these different groups include many individuals with dramatic skill, and others with no small amount of ability as

THE FORTUNE TELLER
(An amateur production)

vocal soloists, what is more natural than that these talents be given an opportunity for expression through the production of amateur opera.

For such a purpose *Pinafore*, *Martha*, *The Chimes of Normandy*, *The Fortune-Teller*, and the more recent *Fire Prince* furnish excellent opportunities for enjoyment to the performers and their audience; and for local "hits" no black-face home-talent show excels *The Mikado* with Ko Ko's "little list" of those who "never will be missed." In addition such productions afford wholesome entertainment for the community, supply a source of revenue for a depleted treasury, and bring the organization anew to the attention of the public,—a recognition which most organizations require for continuity of life. But even more important is the fact that participation in amateur opera by the adults of a community provides an easily accessible and therefore convenient channel through which grown-ups may express themselves musically and dramatically.

IMPORTED DIRECTORS

Semiprofessional producers from commercial schools which train dramatic coaches occasionally offer their services to organizations wishing to give amateur productions. These imported directors frequently supply the music and dramatic material for mixed programs. Since this material is usually commonplace and the charges of such persons are wholly out of proportion to the service rendered, any group will find a more satisfactory and profitable procedure to perfect an organization as suggested in the following chapter, securing from a neighboring city or college town, a musical conductor or a stage manager as may be required. Such a plan will result in a better production of a worthwhile operetta and incidentally in a much larger financial return.

OPERA AS A MUNICIPAL PROJECT

Just as amateur opera serves the individual units of a community through its clubs and different organizations, so, in turn, it may become a municipal project and serve as a practical means by which a city may furnish wholesome entertainment to its citizens. For example, the city of St. Louis has evolved a plan by which for eight seasons it has presented what may be termed "opera by the people and for the people"—that is, opera on a non-profit basis and at extremely low cost to those who pay—to say nothing of some twelve hundred free admissions which are usually dispensed during each season. By combining its musical and civic forces in a similar way, any small city may, by utilizing its amateur talent, accomplish the same result. The only requisites are a municipal auditorium or an ample outdoor stage, a board of guarantors, and a capable opera director.

There are at present in the United States some fifteen cities with an average population of fifteen thousand people, spending approximately $5,000 each year for municipal music, most of which is in the form of band concerts. Part of this fund might most advantageously be spent for one or two productions of opera—productions which would add variety and attraction to the season's music program. In producing amateur opera under civic auspices it may be that in some small cities certain organizations will include in their membership a sufficient number of people to stage the production without assistance from members of other organizations; the wise director, however, who has charge of the production of amateur "municipal" opera in a small city will not limit his personnel to a single group, but will draw upon the entire community for his chorus, principals, and his corps of assistants. By including representatives from various organizations he will secure helpful cooperation and healthful competition, and will produce an opera which will have for the participants the added interests of new contacts. Moreover, such a production should attract a much larger and more varied audience than would an opera which included only the membership of a single organization. But, however presented, amateur opera is a vehicle which should not be overlooked by any city which wishes to develop a spirit of cooperation and a sense of musical appreciation among its citizens—in a pleasant, wholesome, and worthwhile way.

ART FOR ART'S SAKE

It has just been said that municipal opera might be termed "opera by the people and for the people." It may seem a far cry to "aristocratic music for aristocrats" or "art for art's sake," but such is what one might term some of the projects which are being sponsored and supported in larger cities by certain groups of people who are primarily and ultimately interested in one thing, namely, art for the sake of art alone. No urge for money-making, no incentive to please a capricious public, no striving for prestige from the taking of leading parts, enter into the productions of such a group. Every player and every detail is subservient to the one idea—art. A good example of such an organization is that of the Fine Arts Society of Detroit. This is an organization of more than twenty years' standing. Its membership, active and associate, numbers three hundred and fifty and for years it has had a long waiting list. This society gives five or six private performances each year to members and guests. The programs include some operas, as well as one-act plays, pageants, and other forms of drama. *Robin Hood*, *Iolanthe*, and *San Toy* are among the operas which have been included in their programs. Might not the success of this society lure other groups in other localities to make a similar effort to utilize the opera in what is, perhaps, its most idealistic and most effective presentation?

CONCLUSION

In conclusion, then, may we not say that amateur opera may be made just as valuable a form of expression for the adults in a community as is the operetta for children in the grades and high school?   Whether it function in the hands of a single organization or in the hands of a combined group of organizations,—whether it be dressed in the ordinary clothes of a municipal project or whether it be apparelled in the raiment befitting an art-for-art's-sake production— amateur opera provides a medium through which adults may satisfy their desires for accomplishment along musical and dramatic lines.   Therefore, as individuals and as communities, we should see to it that the musical appreciation and interest which have been aroused and fostered in the school be kept alive and developed by being turned into one of the natural channels of a mature form of expression— amateur opera.

CHAPTER IV

Plan of Organization

As he faces the many details, the person in charge, whom we shall call the director, will find that two courses of procedure are open: first, a single-handed production in which he himself will have to assume all of the responsibility and do most of the work; second, a partnership procedure, in which he will select a number of assistants, each of whom will assume some definite responsibility and work under his supervision.

Frequently the director, particularly if he be an inexperienced supervisor, selects the first plan because of its apparent simplicity. He may argue that it will be easier to assume all of the responsibility and to give his time and energy after school hours to rehearsals than it will be to arouse the interest and secure the cooperation of others. Again he may reason that to ask for help from the other departments may be interpreted as an evidence of his own limited ability. The young director is inclined to trust in his own capacity for work beyond his ability for organization. Were he sure, however, of his ability to select and to direct assistants, the average director would welcome the help which the cooperative plan affords.

AN ALL-SCHOOL PROJECT

Notwithstanding the hesitancy of inexperienced directors to adopt the partnership plan when staging a school operetta, experience has proved that this procedure not only expedites the preparation of the operetta, but that it favorably affects the school as a whole. Moreover, though the experienced director may have presented many operettas with little or no assistance, he will find if he adopts the co-operative method, that he has produced, with less effort, a performance of a uniform quality of excellence hitherto unachieved by him; and that, as an executive, he has gained new and valuable experience. For "the preparation and staging of an operetta in an adequate fashion affords a training as valuable as a semester of college work," testifies a supervisor of several years' successful experience, and particularly is this remark true when the cooperative procedure has been followed.

Other departments, moreover, will be interested in the plan, and the partnership method will convert the operetta into an all-school project, a project which will secure from the outset the interest and assistance of the various departments, the principal, and the superintendent.

THE PREPARATION

The director who is staging an operetta for the first time will gain a more definite conception of just what is to be done in connection with the preparation and final performance of an operetta, just what steps he will need to take, if he studies the operetta carefully and makes specific notes, in outline form, of the main points to be worked out. Such an outline should read somewhat as follows:

   I. MUSIC: 1. Chorus   2. Solos   3. Accompaniment
  II. PRINCIPALS: 1. Try-outs   2. Understudies
 III. LINES: 1. Memorization   2. Prompting
  IV. ACTING: (a) For principals; (b) For chorus 1. Exits, entrances, etc.   2. Groupings   3. Pantomime   4. Dances
   V. COSTUMES: 1. Principals   2. Chorus
  VI. MAKE-UP
 VII. STAGE: 1. Physical conditions   2. Scenery   3. Properties   4. Lighting   5. Special effects
VIII. REHEARSALS: 1. Individual   2. Cast   3. Chorus   4. General
  IX. BUSINESS DETAILS: 1. Advertising   2. Tickets   3. Programs

After a study of this rather formidable list, the inexperienced producer will perhaps need no further argument to convince him of the desirability of the cooperative plan.

THE GENERAL DIRECTOR

Let no one make the mistake, however, of thinking that an operetta can be successfully *produced* by a board of directors. It should be definitely understood at the outset that the authority and the chief responsibility for the preparation and final performance rest with one person—namely, the person in charge, the general director. This person must be an individual who understands people, who can work with them, who has an abundance of energy and patience, and what is more important, who is so filled with enthusiasm that he communicates it to his assistants, to the cast, and to the chorus. In the smaller grade schools and in the rural or consolidated high school, the supervisor will probably have to assume the larger share of the preparation; and if he has not had special training, he will find that he can use to advantage whatever knowledge he may have acquired of drama, drawing and colors, and costume design.

SHARING RESPONSIBILITIES

The director, if wise, will first determine how much of the preparation he will be able to delegate to others. He should understand that no matter how small the hamlet in which he may be located, he will be sure to find some persons who are able and ready to assist him. In choosing such assistants he will do well to consider only those persons who are able to take suggestions as well as to offer helpful comments. When the supervisor as a director is selecting a corps of helpers, he will consider first, faculty members; next, capable students; and finally, persons in the community who have interest and ability in some special phase of the operetta

—such as painting of scenery, designing of costumes, or directing of stage business.

The director of amateur opera in the community, however, will follow the reverse procedure; he will consider first, the individuals in the community; then the students of the high school who will not only be able to render real service but who will also interest the entire student body in the performance; and finally, the members of the school faculty. To both the supervisor-director and the amateur director the various departments in the school will furnish valuable help,—departments such as Art, Dramatics, Commerce, English, Home Economics, Manual Training, Physics, Physical Training, Speech, Geography, and History.

PERSONNEL

When the personnel of the school and community includes a wide and varied list of capable persons, the supervisor-director or the amateur director will be able to secure a complete corps of assistants. An ideal organization will include the following:

	Music—in charge of Conductor—	Chorus / Soloists / Accompanist / Orchestra
*GENERAL DIRECTOR	Stage and action—in charge of Stage Manager and Assistant—	Principals / Chorus / Carpenter / Costume Mistress / Property Man / Electrician
	Business—in charge of Business Manager and Assistant—	Finance / Advertising / House details

*In most school productions, the supervisor will act in the dual capacity of General Director and Conductor; frequently he will also assume the duties of Stage Manager.

Briefly stated, the duties of these persons are as follows:

CONDUCTOR

The entire responsibility for the music will be carried by the conductor. In most school operettas this person will be the supervisor and in community productions the director. Some of the work will be delegated to assistants, but the preparation of solos, choruses, and accompaniment will be made by the conductor.

STAGE MANAGER

In general, the stage manager's duties will include the supervision of all of the dramatic details of the production; the stage, scenery, properties, lighting, costumes, make-up, and the stage business, that is, the action of the cast and chorus; specifically, he will coach the spoken lines of the operetta and direct all of the dramatic action. When a person of experience can be found who will take over the responsibilities of the stage manager, the director will find such help to be of distinct advantage at general rehearsals and at the final performance, when he himself, as conductor, must be in the pit with the baton. If the director does act as stage manager, he should appoint an assistant, whose duties are outlined in Chapter XVII.

STAGE CARPENTER

The stage carpenter will have as his chief responsibility the scenery and the fixed physical conditions of the stage as a whole. If new scenery is to be painted or old scenery rebuilt, such work will be done by him or under his direct supervision. To him will be assigned the construction of any large stage properties which may be needed, such as walls, stairways, gates, stumps, etc. He will direct the setting and removal of scenery and will arrange for a scene shifting rehearsal prior to the general rehearsals.

PROPERTY MAN

The property man will have as his responsibility the assembling and arranging for the rehearsals and final performance all of the properties, other than the scenery, which go to make up the stage settings.   He will see to it that all small paraphernalia, such as papers, telephone, dishes, etc., are in their right places on the stage or ready for the use of the individual actors at the proper time.   A reliable person, preferably one who is not taking part in the production, should be selected for this position.

COSTUME MISTRESS

The costume mistress will have the responsibility of caring for the costumes.   If these are rented from a professional costumer, it will be necessary for her to examine the entire shipment upon its arrival and to verify the several items on the bill with the original order.   She will then check out these costumes to the various members of the cast and chorus, making sure that all outfits are complete and that they fit satisfactorily.   At the close of the dress rehearsal, and later, at the final performance, all costumes will be checked in by her and she will supervise the packing of them for their return to the costumer.

When the costumes are made by the parents or the domestic art class, they should be brought to the costume mistress for inspection.

ELECTRICIAN

The electrician will have charge of the lighting.   It will be his duty to secure the proper supply of colored bulbs, gelatine slides for the flood-lights, and to locate properly and adjust the border-lights and footlights.   He will also be responsible for making, or having made, all of the electrical appliances to be used throughout the production.   After having had special lighting rehearsals with the stage manager, he will operate the switch board and any other electrical equipment which may be used during the dress rehearsal and the final performance.

THE BUSINESS MANAGER

The business manager should look after all of the financial details connected with the production. He should handle all advertising and arrange for the publication of advance news stories, the latter to be written, preferably, by the English department. He should cooperate with the art department in devising effective posters. He will attend to the printing of programs and tickets, and arrange for the box-office sales. All bills will be paid by him after they have been properly approved. The teacher of commerce or a capable student will make an efficient business manager in the school production.

ASSIGNING DUTIES

Having determined upon the best available persons for the several positions discussed, the director should next meet each assistant individually and go over carefully with him the various details as previously enumerated. He should next call a general meeting of all the staff, in order to go through the operetta in a sketchy manner, and to give each person an idea of it as a whole. Each assistant should be given a typewritten outline of his duties, as agreed upon, and the director should likewise have a copy. At this first meeting, the date of the final performance should be decided upon, and a schedule of rehearsals arranged which will give fair consideration to the preparation of the operetta and to the programs of other departments of the school. In the case of amateur opera a date must be decided upon which will not conflict with important events already scheduled.

HARMONY IN ORGANIZATION

In dealing with his assistants the director should see to

it that no differences of opinion occur to mar the pleasant relationships which existed at the beginning of the study of the operetta. Friction often arises from a lack of definite understanding on the part of the cast, the chorus, or the corps of assistants as to the specific duties which have been assigned to each; or it may occur because of some individual's failure to recognize the authority of a certain assistant. For instance, the conductor may, during a rehearsal, criticize or completely reverse some part of the action which the dramatic coach, acting as stage manager, has carefully worked out. Or, again, the property man may presume to dictate to the stage carpenter in regard to some detail of the stage setting. Unpleasant incidents of this sort seriously affect the morale of the entire group. If the director is diplomatic, however, he may do much to prevent their occurrence, or if not actually to prevent them, at least to smooth them out when they do occur. Should trouble seem imminent, should someone balk in the rehearsal, for instance, in the last scene of Act I, the director will avoid an open break by taking up another scene, leaving the preceding one for another rehearsal. If the director possesses a reasonable amount of tact, humor, and consideration, he will be able to direct his assistants and cast efficiently to cope with any difficult situation that may arise, and to maintain a harmonious relationship with all concerned throughout the rehearsals and final performance.

ACKNOWLEDGING ASSISTANCE

Since these various assistants will render valuable help from the outset it will be courteous as well as wise for the person in charge of the publicity to make an early announcement of their names, together with their responsibilities. Furthermore, when the programs are printed, the director should see that their services are duly acknowledged.

Not only, then, should the director know how to select a

good operetta, but he must, in addition, be familiar with the various phases of preparation. He will then divide among competent people the responsibility of this preparation, so that, when the final performance is given, no detail will have been overlooked.

CHAPTER V

Choosing an Operetta

INFLUENCE AND IMPORTANCE

It is only necessary to take into consideration the influence which an operetta inevitably has upon its performers and upon the audience to realize that too much care cannot be exercised in the selection of the best material obtainable. Let the director remember that the music of the operetta must be sung many times in preparation for the final performance; and let him realize also that the many hours which must be spent on learning the lines, the music, and the action of the operetta—hours to be taken from many other things —demand a vehicle worthy of that time. Let him keep in mind, too, that the operetta not only supplements or detracts from the standards set up in the class-room, but that it also affects the taste of the pupils and of their audiences.

Again, in the case of the amateur director, the musical taste and standard of his group or community are in some measures indicated by the opera selected. Furthermore, let the director of the school operetta or of the amateur opera understand that when he selects an operetta for public performance he virtually places his own stamp of approval on it. If the supervisor or amateur director, then, realizes and accepts his responsibility and opportunity in connection with the selection of an operetta, he will be confronted by two questions: first, "What will the singer do to the operetta?"—second, and equally important, "What will the operetta do to the singer?"

DEARTH OF GOOD MATERIAL

In no other field of school music is there a greater dearth

of good material or so wide a variation in quality as there is in the field of the operetta. "There are no good operettas," say some of our prominent supervisors, in explanation of their practice of producing few or no operettas. It is, unfortunately, only too true that the growth and popularity of this type of entertainment has led to the publication of a large number of operettas, and it is a cause for regret that so many of them, consisting of cheap and tawdry verses set to commonplace and drab, or jazz-colored melodies, masquerade as worthy operettas, and as such are admitted into good standing in the musical repertoire of many schools. It has been stated by conservative persons that about one school operetta in ten is really worth while; others put the percentage much lower.

In view of this situation, the careful supervisor and the amateur director with musical ideals will realize that, after all, the choice of an operetta is not a trivial matter. For in his choice of the operetta as of all music material, he takes his own measure; he reveals his musical standards, his thoroughness in searching out good material, and his ability to discriminate between worth-while and mediocre operettas and operas. If he be jealous of his own reputation and chary about the music which he selects, he will adopt an attitude which is just the reverse of the court which assumes a person innocent until proved guilty; that is, he will consider each operetta questionable until he has tested it and proved its worth. Needless to say, such a method of cautious selection will not only safeguard his own reputation as a musician, but will also add one blow to the doom of the mediocre and worthless operetta.

ARE GOOD OPERETTAS POSSIBLE?

The assertion that there are no good operettas at once raises a question which is pertinent—that is, "Do inherent conditions within the operetta itself preclude or limit the

quality of excellence which should characterize it?"   It is
contended by some persons that because of its dramatic
element it is impossible to provide the operetta with lines
and music which are of equal merit with those of the cantata.
And it is still further objected that operettas, like opera, are
ineffective and inartistic because they are a combination of
arts.   On this last point it may be enlightening to note what
Clive Bell says in his book on Art.   "I cannot consider anything a work of art," he writes "to which I cannot react
emotionally."   Just as we have in painting a combination
of form and color to which we respond emotionally, so we
have in the operetta a combination of form, color, movement,
melody, and poetry to which we give an emotional response.

A moment's reflection will make clear the fact that each
of the elements which go to make up the operetta is susceptible of a high degree of excellence.   For example, the
verses of an operetta may be written in good English; the
plot may be as reasonable and as well developed as that of a
good play; and the music of the solos and choruses may be
good melodies, harmonized with as interesting progressions
as those of the cantata.   With these separate elements in
combination, then, it is entirely possible to have a composition as a whole that is worthy of the study of the performers
and the attention of the audience.   Should we not therefore
grant to that large group of average citizens to whom post-
impressionism and the whole-tone scale mean nothing, and
who today are making their choice between the ever-present
talkies and jazz supplied in mass production, the enjoyment
also of worth-while operetta and other forms of art in which
their children or they themselves may participate?

INDEPENDENCE IN CHOOSING

In connection with the school operetta it may be said that
only a few supervisors really select their own operettas; for

the great majority of them merely accept material that has been thrust upon their attention by convincingly written advertisements accompanied by attractive illustrations of stage settings. Still others rely upon the financial success of an operetta which has been given in a neighboring town, and again others order another operetta by Mr. Blank, simply because an operetta by this composer has previously been given and has proved a financial success. The experienced supervisor who selects an operetta which is poor, trifling, and commonplace, should have a session of soul-searching inquiry and propound to himself the question: "*Why* am I teaching music?" The inexperienced supervisor, however, may be excused if the standard of his first operetta is not all that it should be. Discrimination comes with experience. One must have lived much with music, have thought much about music, and have caught the inner spirit of music to be able to choose wisely an operetta which has musical value.

Proceeding from the assumption that the best is none too good and that his community will appreciate an operetta of real merit, the conscientious supervisor will begin his search early—weeks or it may be months in advance. A fruitful field will be opened by sending out frank letters of inquiry to supervisors of experience, who are known to have high musical standards, asking the names of operettas to which they can give their endorsement. The supervisor may then write to music publishers of recognized standing for a selection of the best operettas which they have published. With his material before him, the director will soon discover in his first cursory examination of some operettas that a few pages are sufficient to brand them as unworthy of consideration. When he has eliminated the less suitable operettas, he should go through very thoroughly those remaining which appear to have merit, and should weigh them in a critical manner according to severe standards.

STEPS IN CHOOSING

In making his selection the director should apply certain tests to each operetta which he examines. He must make a careful test for adaptability, and he must also make a three-fold test for quality—that is, quality of text, quality of plot, an quality of music. In determining the adaptability of an operetta, the supervisor, or director, keeping in mind the age and ability of his group of singers, must ask himself whether the words and music are suitable; whether the vocal requirements are within the range of his singers' voices; whether, in the case of the school operetta, it is arranged suitably as to the number of parts—unison, two, three, or four part; whether the number and character of the solo parts and the chorus requirements can be managed; and he must also determine whether the demands of the production from the physical side, that is, the scenery, the lighting, the number of costumes called for, and the possibilities of the stage at his disposal, can be properly taken care of; and finally, he will consider the operetta from the standpoint of the audience.

QUALITY OF TEXT

In making his tests for quality, the director should first examine the text scrupulously, reading aloud all the dialogue and lyrics. Is the English good or commonplace? Is it poetic or trivial? Are there any questionable speeches? Would the dialogue read well in an English class? Are there parts which are worth memorizing? In making this evaluation of the operetta, the supervisor will find that the assistance of a good teacher of English will be invaluable to him.

QUALITY OF PLOT

In determining the quality of the plot the director may ask himself: Does the story develop in a life-like manner?

Is it sincere and genuine? Are the situations natural? Is the plot as a whole well constructed? Does each scene lead naturally and easily into the next one? Are the characters interesting and well drawn? Are the descriptions picturesque? Is there occasion for the play of the imagination? Is there movement throughout the story? Is there a reasonable amount of action, and is it well suited to the lines? Does the plot contain the element of humor or of lightheartedness in a sufficient degree to lift the operetta above a too-serious level? In fine, with certain minor changes and the omission of the music, could the operetta be successfully presented as a play? In this matter the supervisor will do well to consult the teacher of dramatics.

QUALITY OF MUSIC

In a similar way one should test the quality of the music. Has it real merit? Is it worth memorizing? Is the melody beautiful or ordinary; pleasing or uninteresting; tuneful or trivial? Is the impression made by the text and intensified by the music a worthy one? Is the harmonic background colorful and imaginative? Are the progressions natural? Are certain modulations frequently repeated,—even "dragged in by the heels" sometimes? Does the accompaniment consist of straight chords or has it variety; does it offer possibilities for instrumentation?

If the director applies the foregoing tests to the operetta under consideration, if he seriously asks himself these suggested questions about the text, plot, and music, he will be in little danger of selecting a mediocre or uninteresting operetta.

CLASSIFICATION OF OPERETTAS
Group I, Poor

In this group we find those operettas which are but little better than the old slapstick comedy-movies, the distinctly poor operettas;—and unfortunately by far the greater number of school operettas of today fall into this class. The lines are nothing more than veritable drivel, and the music little more than mere pitch and rhythm. An illustration of the verse of one of these operettas will show how utterly banal and worthless are the operettas of this group.

> "Once we had a darling little sister"
> (Chorus   .   .   .   .   "Sister")
> "The joy and sunlight of our happy home"
> (Chorus   .   .   .   .   "Our happy home")
> "You can sure imagine how we've missed her"
> (Chorus   .   .   "Yes, we've missed her")
> "Since dear Annie sought the world to roam."

Group II, Mediocre

In the operettas of this group we find that the music corresponds to that of the ultra-popular song type. The verses are mere doggerel, even poorer than those of the cheapest musical comedy. Because the inferiority of this group of operettas is less apparent than that of the absolutely poor group, its influence is perhaps more insidious and therefore more harmful. The following verse from one of these mediocre operettas when compared with those of a really good operetta shows how much is still left to be desired:

> "Lazily drifting away
> Over the river so bright;
> Wavelets are dashing the spray;
> The moon is the queen of the night.
> The bee, drowsily humming his lay,
> Scents flowers with odors bedight.
> My heart like a bird must away
> To the shore of childhood's delight."

Group III, Good

In the third group—the good operettas—the lines read well and will bear rereading. The verses are *poetry*. Ideas are not forced nor words wrenched to make a rhyme. The music has tuneful melodies and interesting harmonies,—not dissimilar to the music which is used in the class-room. At present there are comparatively few of this group of operettas. They are conservatively advertised and must be sought out. Verses illustrative of this group are:

> "The earth is waking from her rest;
> The lark is on the wing,
> The wind comes blowing from the west
> With news of spring.
> The morning sings with mystic voice;
> Laugh, wind, as larks rejoice!"

Another,

> "Within some unknown garden,
> Mid soft winds blowing free,
> There grows one flower of beauty
> Which blooms alone for me.
> But when unto that fragrant bow'r
> I guide my wandering feet,
> How shall I know the lovely flow'r
> When all are passing sweet?"

And, in lighter vein,

> "Now perhaps you all have wondered
> How I joined the great four hundred
> And acquired a demeanor that is up to date;
> So with kindly condescension
> I will bring to your attention
> A few important facts which I'll accentuate.
> Society! It gives me great anxiety;
> It fills me to satiety;
> It interferes with sobriety;
> If seeking notoriety,
> In infinite variety,
> Just mix up in society;
> That's my advice to you!"

Since, as has been pointed out, there is today an almost overwhelming supply of what may rightly be termed cheap, worthless, and even harmful operettas, and since there are, as compared with this vast number of poor compositions but very few really good ones, it is most apparent that the task of selecting an operetta either for school performance or as a community project is one not to be lightly undertaken. Moreover, since the preparation and the presentation of an operetta leave a definite influence for good or bad on the minds of both its performers and its audience, there is an additional responsibility to be taken into consideration by the director in his selection. But perhaps what is, or what will come to be, the most awakening and the most determining factor influencing the director in making his choice is his own realization that his selection of an operetta actually reveals in unmistakable terms his own musical taste and judgment. When he recognizes these various responsibilities, and when he is willing to spend sufficient time in taking the requisite preliminary steps before making a final selection, then the director need have little fear that the operetta finally decided upon will be suitable to his needs, that it will be entertaining alike to participants and audience, and in all, that it will be well worth the time and work to be expended on it.

CHAPTER VI

Making Necessary Changes in the Operetta

Although the director may have exercised every care in his selection, he will often find that certain changes will better adapt the chosen operetta to his group of actors. For rarely does one find an operetta that is suitable in every particular. Obviously, operettas of the best grade will require fewer changes as compared with those which are mediocre and commonplace. Too often has the performance of an operetta been spoiled for the lack of a blue pencil, —when the director has failed to go through the composition and omit certain parts of the music, lines, or action,—to make necessary additions or changes in the text or music.

OMISSIONS

An amateur performance that is not too long is the exception. Whether or not this condition is due to a slow tempo of the operetta as a whole, it may often be greatly improved by the elimination of some relatively unimportant and unnecessary parts of the music and lines. For instance, it may happen that a principal who has been chosen for his singing ability does not qualify equally well in the delivery of his lines; in this case it will be wise to leave out as many of the actor's speeches as can be omitted without injuring the story as a whole, or interferring with the other spoken parts. Again, the third and fourth stanzas of most solos may often be omitted; and it may sometimes be found— particularly in primary operettas—that one stanza of a solo is sufficient. Occasionally, some part of the action, or even a whole scene, may be spared without seriously impairing the production in its entirety. Especially is this true in the love-scenes of operettas. Such scenes usually serve to em-

barrass the young actors and to amuse the audience.   It is
better, therefore, if such a scene is essential to the story, to
cut the lines as much as possible, to simplify the action, and to
omit entirely any such pantomime as is common to the movies.

ADDITIONS

The director will be alert to discern how and where an
operetta may be better adapted by occasional additions,—
additions to the voices, lines, or characters.   He will find
that this suggestion is particularly applicable to operettas
for the lower grades: for instance, in a primary operetta,
the light voice of a soloist may be supplemented by several
other voices in the background.   In the presentation of
Pandora by C. E. LeMassena, a charming operetta for little
people, the sixth grade composition class of a certain school
took the assignment of writing dialogue, sometimes no
longer than a single speech, for the additional characters,
"Troubles," that were introduced into the story.   The inexperienced director should be warned, however, not to prolong
a scene through the addition of unrelated action or dances.

TRANSPOSITION

Sometimes entire solos or choruses in a primary operetta
are written in too low a key; and occasionally high school
operettas and light operas are unsuited to the range of the
voices available.   Obviously, the remedy lies in transposition.   Furthermore, a change of key often enhances the
musical effect of a composition when voices of a certain
range are lacking and what is even more important, it frequently prevents serious damage to the voices of immature
singers.   Such transposition is often a simple matter and is
less noticeable because of the intervening dialogue which
obviates the necessity of observing any key relationship.
When transposition of the accompaniment and orchestral
parts is necessary it will be found to offer an excellent project for high school music students.

ADAPTATION

Besides the changes within the operetta itself, the director will occasionally find that an operetta may, with some changes, be presented by a group other than the one for which it was written. For example, *Rumpelstiltskin* by Alfred Scott-Gatty, written for high-school students, can be given by intermediate grades with excellent effect,—by adding, perhaps, a few solo voices from the senior high school. Also, *The Feast of the Little Lanterns*, by Paul Bliss, composed for women's voices, can readily be adapted to pupils of intermediate grades, and is greatly enjoyed by them. Likewise certain Grand Operas, including *Martha*,

MARTHA, NANCY, AND SIR TRISTAM
(A normal-school production)

Faust, and *Carmen*, have been made available for presentation by amateur and high school groups through the publication of simplified versions arranged and adapted for non-professional singers.

When the director has made the necessary changes in the operetta which he has selected, in order to adapt it to the ability of its prospective cast, he is then ready for the succeeding steps—the selection and training of the chorus and principals.

CHAPTER VII

Choice and Preparation of Principals

Americans are admittedly obsessed with the idea that the star makes the opera; consequently, in their evaluation of a performance of an opera or operetta, they are inclined to overlook the minor roles, the chorus, and the general ensemble. Fortunately, in amateur and school productions, this overemphasis of principals is less apparent; but it persists even here, to a degree. The non-professional producer, therefore, finds himself confronted with a double responsibility when he selects his cast. He must, in the first place, choose by one method or another those individuals who are best able, in every way, to take the leading parts. At the same time, if he is going to have a well-balanced and consistently good performance, he must use equal discrimination and good judgment in selecting the right persons for those parts which are too often considered of secondary importance—that is, the minor roles and the chorus.

SELECTION OF PRINCIPALS

The selection of principals, which is always of vital importance, is sometimes attended with difficulty. Serious problems may often be avoided, however, if the director will but take into account what solo voices are available, and will then choose an operetta which will provide a suitable vehicle for those voices. Leads should be chosen on merit alone; for social prestige and personality will not compensate for a particular deficiency. In the selection no single requisite should be allowed to determine the choice; in so far as possible each member selected should meet all of the requirements.

The director will usually find it a wise plan to share the responsibility of selecting the principals. For instance, he may find that the teacher of English, or the teacher of dramatics, together with some disinterested musician, will be glad to assist him in making selections.

TRY OUTS

Although there are various ways of selecting principals, the one which is most likely to eliminate politics, appeals of personality, and various "pulls" is that of holding try-outs; this method, which is usually satisfactory to everyone concerned also has the advantage that it may occasionally reveal talent. When the director has decided to use the try-out method, he should, at a sufficiently early date, make an announcement on the bulletin boards and in general assembly, of the date of the try-outs and the selections to be studied. These selections should be, preferably, from the operetta which is to be given.

ALL-SCHOOL SELECTION

One supervisor who has made the grade operetta a successful and integral part of the year's music program has adopted the plan of having all of her pupils memorize, during their class periods, the entire vocal score of the operetta which is to be given. Then, on a date which has been announced previously, she holds, in each grade, try-outs for the principal parts. Before having these preliminary try-outs, however, the supervisor explains to the pupils that in order for their grade to have a possible opportunity to secure final honors, it will be necessary for the students to disregard all personal considerations and to vote for the most competent representative in their grade. The winners from the different grades then try out, and from them a committee of teachers makes the final selection of principals. Such a plan of selection not only relieves the supervisor by placing the responsibility upon the pupils themselves and upon a committee of teachers, but, it also serves to develop in the students an ability to judge with discrimination.

IMPORTED SOLOISTS

High schools or amateur organizations in small towns sometimes find it advisable to use an assisting solo voice from a neighboring city, particularly if the production which is being given includes difficult tenor and soprano roles. When such soloists are chosen, they should possess ability that is clearly beyond that of the local singers, in order that their work may afford an added inspiration to the other members of the cast and to the chorus.

REQUISITES FOR PRINCIPALS

In the selection of principals, it must be borne in mind that there are certain very definite essentials which each principal must have if the operetta, in its final performance, is to be a success.   It may be helpful to list here some of these requisites.

VOICE

The voice of a principal should be adequate for the speaking and singing parts; it should have sufficient carrying power to be heard by the entire audience, particularly by those people who are sitting in the rear of the auditorium.

The matter of sure intonation must also be considered; for a good solo voice, singing sharp or flat under stage surroundings, may often so affect the pitch of the entire chorus that the finale will end in an embarrassing, if not totally unfamiliar, tonality.

DRAMATIC APTITUDE

Each principal selected must possess at least a fair degree of dramatic aptitude; he must have sufficient imagination and ability to give physical expression to the personality and action of the character he is to portray.

ENUNCIATION

In selecting principals, too much stress cannot be put upon the importance of clear enunciation. The principals must enunciate the words of the solos and spoken lines so distinctly that they may be heard plainly by everyone in the audience. Any marked deficiency in the matter of diction should be sufficient grounds for disqualifying anyone from taking a leading role (Cf. Chapter VIII).

DEPENDABILITY

No matter how good a voice a principal may possess, and no matter how much dramatic talent he may display, he will be a hindrance rather than a help to the performance if he cannot be depended upon for regular attendance at rehearsals and for promptness and accuracy in memorizing the lines which have been assigned to him. In other words, each principal must be one who can be depended upon.

SUITABILITY

Finally, if one who is being considered for a leading role qualifies as to vocal ability, dramatic aptitude, enunciation, and dependability, the director must still further consider whether or not he is suitable for the part,—whether he is of the right stature, whether he has the proper bearing, and whether the quality of his voice fits in with the part in question.

UNDERSTUDIES

No director should feel sure of a successful final performance if he has not along with his training of the regular cast coached a group of understudies who are prepared, on short notice, to take the places of any members in leading or minor roles who may—on account of illness or some other unavoidable circumstance—be prevented at the last moment from taking their parts. If the director has chosen his cast by means of try-outs, he will have discovered, through this method, good material for understudies, and will therefore have little difficulty in choosing substitutes and in assigning them to the roles for which they are best qualified. These understudies may also be members of the chorus. They must, however, attend a sufficient number of the cast rehearsals to become thoroughly familiar with the action of the cast. The presence of well-trained understudies also serves another purpose—for the knowledge that someone else stands ready to step into his place acts as an excellent spur to keep each member of the cast alert in the matters of attendance, interest, and effort.

SPONTANEOUS OR DIRECTED ACTION?

The amateur director may adopt one of two methods in developing the dramatic action of the operetta. He may either allow each actor to build his own characterization or he may stimulate the imagination and guide the action of the amateur until it becomes the natural expression of the character portrayed. In every form of expression there may be two or three correct ways of doing things—almost countless wrong ways. Although the wrong way may occur without suggestion, the right ways, except in rare cases, come as the result of explicit direction and repeated drill.

The average music instructor would have little patience with the student who neglects his practice, offering the excuse "music comes to me naturally"; the same instructor, however, in the role of an operetta director proceeds upon the theory that once the amateur comprehends what the scene is about he will spontaneously give a correct interpretation. This assumption temporarily relieves the director but in the end leads to a production that is crude and unfinished.

The necessity of expressing the intended meaning of the writer or composer of a work is as important in the dramatic as in the musical phase of an operetta. No voice teacher would say to his pupil, "Here are your songs; learn them" —and ignore the matter of phrasing or interpretation; not infrequently, however, the director of an operetta follows this very haphazard plan in the preparation of the speaking parts and the action. One instance will illustrate the fallacy of spontaneous interpretation; in a single vocal phrase of a recitative, a page announces the arrival of an expected messenger. He sings, "My Lord, the herald comes!" Having been well set to music, the final word *comes* occurs on the primary accent; and the page should stress this word through a stronger or a longer tone. On the contrary, what a change in meaning occurred when a young singer, inspired by a zealous director to have confidence in his own powers of expression, sang with gusto, "My Lord! the herald comes."

LEARNING THROUGH REPETITION

To the director who has the assistance of a dramatic teacher or coach, the problem is simplified. The directions given in this chapter and in Chapters VIII and XVII will be of assistance to one who must assume without training the responsibilities of a stage manager. Having worked out beforehand *all* of the stage business in detail—just where each property is to be located, where this person is to stand, at what point that character is to take off his hat, in which hand an article is to be held, when this character is to sit down, and so forth—and having read the lines until the meaning is most effectively brought out, the director will by patience and persistent repetition fix all of this stage business in the memories of the several actors. He will furthermore remember that to acquire freedom in any bit of dramatic action the actor should first go through the movements slowly and then fix the action through repetition. Exits and entrances, for example, are most readily learned by walking slowly the last three or the first three steps respectively.

Individual rehearsals with principals, at which time lines will be read and reread to bring out the exact meaning, will conserve the time of the director and speed up the cast and general rehearsals. In the process of giving specific instruction to each actor, the stage manager will be careful not to stifle the individuality of the young actors.

Children, as a rule, are very responsive, and are devoid of self-consciousness; the lights and shades of emotion, whether they be their own or those awakened by their imagination, play easily upon their faces. Good dialogue seldom fails to arouse a sympathetic response from a child, once the words are put into his mouth.

The stage manager may allow each actor first to express himself by word and action; then, if an individual shows interpretative ability, the director will utilize this as a basis from which to develop more complete expression.

Strict adherence to dramatic rules is commonly referred to as of "the old school," of which Bernhardt, Belasco, and Barrymore are examples. The modern trend of dramatics is toward a greater freedom of expression on the part of the individual,—an expression, however, which does not violate the general principles underlying dramatic art. Like the rules of harmony, the rules of dramatic art must be learned before they may be broken; and even then they may be broken only when the end in view can be more naturally and effectively achieved.

STAGE FRIGHT

At a rehearsal prior to the dress rehearsal, the stage manager should make sure that the young actor understands that in the case of a lapse of memory, he should take a few steps to cover the pause required for him to recall the forgotten speech or for the promptor to repeat it to him. Stage fright is often relieved by this same device of changing one's position.   Persons who are inclined toward this failing should be discovered if possible in the early rehearsals and either eliminated or helped to overcome their difficulty. One of the best preventives as well as cures for stage fright —which is only an aggravated case of self-consciousness—is thorough and exact memorization.   Such memorization will serve as a staff upon which the wavering individual may lean and regain a degree of self-assurance and poise.   Another suggestion that is sometimes helpful is to remind the performer that to think of one's self instead of the part he has in the play, really savors of conceit; for, with the exception of parents and immediate friends, the audience is interested, not in Mary, but in the fairy.   The director should urge such individuals particularly to "play their parts."

FIRST CAST REHEARSAL

The chief aim of the first rehearsal of the principals should be to give to the actors the meaning of the story as a whole; following this, the central thought of each separate scene should be brought out.   After the actors have a general idea of the operetta, the various members of the cast should read aloud the lyrics and the lines, each character reading his own part.   At this first rehearsal the stage manager should impress upon the cast the fact that the spoken lines must receive relatively as much attention as the songs.   It is not enough that the words of the lines be memorized; the amateur should learn that the first step in memorization is to understand the meaning.   Failure in this regard may result in tragic or humorous situations: for example, in *Pinafore*, Ralph Rackstraw, an ordinary seaman who has developed a love for the Captain's daughter, says, "True I lack birth"—to which the Boatswain remarks,

"You've a berth on this very ship." The latter line was once delivered with gusto by a boy of uncertain memory as follows: "You've got a bed on this here boat." At this first rehearsal general suggestions with reference to tone, diction, and stage deportment should be given. This preliminary training will serve to lessen considerably the work which will later be required for individual rehearsals.

TRAINING OF THE PRINCIPALS

The principals, individually and in small groups, should be regularly trained and rehearsed first in the music and lines and then in the action, by either the stage manager or the dramatic coach. In case this is done by the stage manager, he will be helped by the suggestions in Chapters x and xvii. After the principals are thoroughly familiar with their songs, their lines, and their stage business, then and only then should they take part with the chorus in a general rehearsal.

CHAPTER VIII

Suggestions for the Amateur Actor

Familiarity with dramatic action comes only through study and observation of stage production at close range. Ability to do individually those various things which go to make up dramatic action—movement, gesture, and groupings, technically known as stage business—is acquired only through a broad actual experience and under expert direction. There are, however, certain fundamentals of dramatic action with which every amateur director and young actor should be acquainted. Notwithstanding the importance of these fundamentals both to principals and chorus, they are frequently disregarded by amateur directors who substitute for them a vague and heterogeneous procedure which they term spontaneous action. Some of these fundamentals we shall consider for the benefit of those persons who may not have had the opportunity for observation and experience in the field of dramatics.

HOW TO STAND

The matter of posture should receive the careful attention of every director. Correct posture is essential not only because of its bearing upon the actor's appearance, but also on account of its influence upon the voice in speech and song. The progressive supervisor will have given this subject attention at rehearsals of glee club and chorus; if, however, it has been neglected, it should be repeatedly emphasized throughout the preparation of the operetta.

Correct posture is best illustrated by the position of the head and body of a person who is carrying a weight balanced upon the head.   It will be observed that the head is held over the spine with chin drawn backward, but not raised; the chest leads; the abdominal wall is slightly retracted; the tips of the shoulders are low—in the position assumed when there are weights in the hands; the shoulder blades are flat against the back; and the weight of the body is on the balls of the feet.

HOW TO WALK

To take a few steps across the stage in a manner that appears perfectly natural is rarely done without repeated rehearsals.   Contrary to opinion, this ability to walk properly on the stage is not an unimportant matter.   Because the stage is on a level with the eyes of the audience, the various movements of the actor are unusually prominent.   Negatively considered, the most common faults which are noticeable in the stage movements of amateurs are: maintaining a tense, rigid carriage; carrying the head thrown far back, and protruding the chest; thrusting the head forward instead of holding it over the spinal column; swaying and twisting the hips; walking in a mincing fashion, or with short, hesitant steps.   In walking, the correct upright posture should be maintained, the weight shifted from the balls of the feet alternately, the shoulders and hips relatively motionless, and the arms swinging in a restricted but easy fashion.   In walking, as in standing, the heels should be employed only as a secondary means of maintaining balance and carrying the weight of the body.

HOW TO COME ON THE STAGE

The exact manner in which each actor comes upon the stage is determined somewhat by the nature of the scene into which he enters.   Every actor, however, follows one general rule: the up-stage foot, the foot farthest from the audience, is the one to be set upon the stage first.   For example: *A* enters from the right (as the audience looks at the stage) ; his right foot, therefore, is the "up-stage" foot, the one with which he should make his entrance. The amateur who is playing a "character" part should suit his entrance to the spirit of the scene and to the emotion demanded by his particular part.

HOW TO LEAVE THE STAGE

When the actor is about to leave the stage, he should so space his steps that as he passes into the exit his up-stage foot is advanced, and the weight of his body is thrown upon it. If *A* makes his exit through the same door from which he entered, the up-stage foot—this time the left foot— should lead. Possibly the stage business may necessitate his turning back toward some one whom he is leaving on the stage, in which case he will, as he turns around, pivot on the down-stage foot, shifting his weight as he does so; at this point he is using his up-stage foot for balance. Having delivered his speech, he will pivot again and make his exit on his up-stage foot.

In character parts, which as has been said are exceptions, the preceding rule may not always hold. For example, the soldier who is about to exit may turn and snap his heels together as he salutes; the butler may place his heels together in a precise fashion and bow; in each case, however, the exit is completed on the up-stage foot. If the principals in a children's operetta are taught that they should always keep the face turned toward the audience, the technic of entrances and exits will have been cared for.

HOW TO SIT DOWN

As the actor stands by the chair in which he is to sit, his feet—one slightly advanced—should be separated at an angle of about forty-five degrees; the weight of his body should be thrown on the foot nearest the chair, and the body

should be lowered deliberately. The actor should sit easily
in the chair, usually keeping the spine erect. These directions are, of course, for those who play "straight" parts, in
contrast to "character" roles, which require their own peculiar technique.

HOW TO RISE

When the actor rises, he should throw the weight of his
body on to the foot which is advanced, raising his weight
with the back foot. He should avoid raising his body by
pressing down with his hands upon the chair; nor should
he lean forward, as does the aged man.

WHERE TO LOOK

Amateurs seem to find an inexplicable fascination in the
floor. Possibly this habit of looking down is caused by the
self-consciousness which arises when they find themselves on
the professional side of the footlights. To maintain the
reality of a scene, the actor should look outside the footlights
rather than confine his gaze to the narrow limits of the
stage; he should look at or beyond the audience; but manifestly not *at* anyone in the audience. During dialogue between two people, the actors should never gaze directly into
each other's eyes; such a procedure is very disconcerting.
The actor should focus the eyes just above or beyond the
person addressed and when he makes an "aside" or "solo"
speech, he directs his gaze as though the audience were on
a level with his own eyes. When the actor speaks or sings
he should keep his face toward the audience; if he does not
face straight front, he should present at least a three-quar-
ter's view. When he speaks to someone up-stage, that is, to
one who stands more or less behind him, the actor should
turn, to some extent, but not to such a degree as to prevent
the audience from hearing his voice and seeing his facial
expression.

HOW TO KNEEL

When the actor kneels on both knees, he may face the audience, or he may assume a diagonal position; in extreme cases he may even turn his back to the audience. When he kneels on one knee, if he faces in any direction other than "straight front," he should kneel on the "down-stage" knee, the knee nearest to the audience (Cf. Chapter IX).

GESTURE AND PANTOMINE

Gesture is the use of attitudes and movements of the body to express definite ideas and emotions. To be effective, gesture should be used sparingly and for a specific purpose. It is employed in solo speeches, in dialogue, and occasionally in song.

Pantomime is a comprehensive term which includes both gesture and facial expression.

THE HANDS

It is relatively easy to attain a graceful position of the hands, yet few take the trouble to acquire it. The young actor will be helped if he will study the reproductions and photographs of the old Greek sculptors; they are faultless. The amateur should practice until the first, or index finger, rises naturally above the second and third fingers. This finger is always used to indicate or to point out; if it is slightly separated from and raised above the other fingers it gives force and vitality to the hand. The second and third fingers, called by the Greeks, "husband and wife," should be held close together. The little finger, if allowed to follow its own inclination, is apt to droop or curl; it should therefore be held a little apart from the second and third fingers and almost straight out. The thumb should not be allowed to curl or turn inward; it should be held out and away from the palm. After a brief period of practice, the amateur will not only acquire the proper position of the hands and the ability to use them effectively in gesture, but he will soon gain that degree of physical control which will enable him to use his hands correctly with unconscious ease and assurance.

RUTH CHATTERTON in *MARIE ROSE*
(An illustration of expressive hands)

GESTURE OF SIMPLE LOCATION

The gesture of location is more frequently used than any other, and is employed to point out a person or place. The relative position of the fingers follows the lines of the old Greek statues. The hand, with the palm turned down, is

DIANA FROM THE VATICAN MUSEUM
(Note graceful curve in arms—faultless hands)

directed toward the object, person, or the place designated. This gesture should be practiced as related to, or indicating locations on, four levels: (1) on a level with the floor; (2) on a level with the waist; (3) on a level with the shoulders; (4) on a level above the head; also in three angles: straight front, diagonally front, and to the side.

The gesture of location is begun by moving the arm rather slowly toward the front of the body until the elbow, which is turned slightly outward, is close to but just past the hip; meanwhile the forearm is raised *in front of and across* the body until it attains the desired level and approximates a right angle to the upper-arm; the gesture is completed by extending the forearm toward the object which is to be pointed out. It should be noted that the arm is extended, not rigidly straight but only so far as to retain the natural beauty of the arm when it is slightly flexed. The palm is underneath but the hand does not droop; instead, it should have an attitude of vitality and force, an attitude which is emphasized by the thumb and the little finger when they are separated from the others, and particularly by the index finger as it specifically designates the thing pointed out.

In a salute of honor, which is given by raising the hand above the head or in front of the body, the gesture should begin in the same manner as does the gesture of location.

GESTURE OF APPEAL

The gesture of appeal is another gesture which every amateur may well spend time to acquire. The chief distinction between the gesture of location and the gesture of appeal lies in the position of the palm. In appeal, the palm is held *up*, ready to receive the thing for which the actor is asking. A gesture of appeal may express varying degrees of emotion; it may be called forth by the child asking for something of slight importance, or it may be prompted by the passionate craving of the condemned man pleading for that reprieve which promises life. Generally speaking, the use of one hand is sufficient to emphasize this emotion.

THE TIMING OF GESTURE

A gesture may be made with the perfection of a Bernhardt and yet fail utterly of its purpose if it be not properly timed. Every bit of dramatic action, particularly that of gesture, must be exactly timed to the speech or emotion

which is the occasion for its use.   In order to emphasize the
full meaning of a speech, the gesture must be made at the
instant when the vital word of a line is uttered.   Just as the
absence of precision in attack detracts from the effect of a
musical phrase, so a tardy gesture weakens the dramatic
action of the moment.   On the other hand, an action must
not *anticipate* the word or emotion with which it is associated.
For example, the little fairy is hiding behind a toadstool;
to the audience she is plainly visible, but when the play-
children come onto the stage, they must *search* to discover
her.   They know exactly where she is—she has been in that
identical spot at every rehearsal; if they are good little
actors, however, they will *discover* her on the night of the
performance at the *right instant*, after a careful search in
all other directions.   Such bits of action, very accurately
timed, are the basis of that real technique which catches the
attention and holds the interest of an audience.   If proof
were needed one has but to recall the impression of terror
which the veteran professional creates when on the night of
the hundredth performance he discovers the fateful telegram
on his table.

RESPONSE TO GESTURE

To be effective, a gesture should be held until the other
actor or actors have—in the terms of the movie—"regis-
tered" a response to the idea or emotion expressed by the
gesture.   In the case of solo speeches, the actor should hold
the gesture long enough for the audience to grasp the idea
or realize the emotion which his gesture expresses.   The following examples will illustrate: A traveller exclaims, "Look,
a band of gypsies is coming down the road!"   As he speaks
the actor glances toward the person he is addressing to make
sure that he has attracted his attention; next, he points
(gesture of location) toward the place where the gypsies are
supposed to be seen; and at the same time his eyes follow the

direction in which he points.   Again, "Halt, and give the countersign!" the sentry on duty calls to the unknown person who is advancing through the darkness.   He points his gun at the intruder and sights along the barrel ready to fire if necessary.   He holds this position until the stranger responds to his command.   The force of such a gesture is lost if as soon as he speaks his lines the sentry lowers his gun.   In actual life this action might result in a tragedy; for the soldier on the stage it destroys that dramatic atmosphere which his action should create.

In Act I of *The Fire Prince* by Hadley, Alphonso and Enrico, brothers of the Prince, enter the grounds of the summer palace, where a history lesson is in progress.   Suddenly they discover the Duchess, an honorary governess, in a window overlooking the plaza; and in the mock style of a troubadour, Alphonso, after thrumming an imaginary guitar, sings to her: "I see my love at the casement high! She waits for a sign from me!"   The gesture of location is effectively employed on the first line; it begins by raising the arm on "love," reaches the climax on "casement," and is held through the word "high"; the hand is then easily lowered to the side during the delivery of the succeeding words.   There is no reason for holding the gesture, for the idea has been expressed.

GESTURE FOR EMPHASIS

A comparatively brief speech may be greatly strengthened by the use of several gestures.   For instance, at the close of the same act of *The Fire Prince*, Prince Prigio, who has been disinherited and left alone by the King and his Court, has a soliloquy which opens: (1) "Disinherited! (2) no money; (3) no clothes but these I wear; (4) no means of locomotion; (5) cold rice pudding—"   This speech which leads immediately into an unusual Finale may be given greater emphasis if accompanied by the following gestures: (1) right hand to

head; (2) both palms up, hands extended; (3) downward sweep of the hands from chest to hips, palms up; (4) negative shake of the head; (5) both hands pushing away an imaginary dish and the face slightly averted. The effectiveness of these gestures is dependent upon the discontinuance of each gesture as soon as the idea for which it was used has been expressed.

MASTER GESTURE

Character parts are often more effective if a specific gesture or a characteristic mannerism is used by the player throughout the performance; the saucy servant girl stands with arms akimbo, and the dignified man of affairs folds his arms across his chest.

DICTION

Even more important than gesture is the matter of diction. If an audience were asked whether they had enjoyed the performance of an operetta, their decision would be determined largely by whether or not they had been able to hear the words. And this is rightly so; for an audience is, or should be, a company of hearers.

The operetta includes so large an amount of music that it is an easy matter for the director to give too little attention to the spoken lines. No extended argument is necessary to make plain the fact that any speech of an actor which is not understood is a distinct detriment to the entire production. Important details in the plot are often revealed in the spoken lines. A single illustration will suffice.

In *The Mikado*, before referred to, Nanki-Poo, son of the Mikado is disguised as a minstrel. He reveals the fact during the opening scene that Ko-Ko, recently appointed Lord High Executioner and betrothed to Yum-Yum, with whom Nanki is deeply in love, has been condemned to death for flirting. This fact, which is also mentioned in the succeeding speech, is not only the cue for the solo which follows but it is also the occasion for many of the extremely comic situations which later develop.   At one performance of this opera, a timid Nanki, whose opening speeches were inaudible, and a Pish-Tush with a cavernous diction, completely concealed the interesting and important fact that the crime which Ko-Ko had committed was flirting—and so partially spoiled a scene that was, from a musical standpoint, excellent.

THE USE OF VOWELS

The acquisition of perfect diction is a matter of extended training.   A knowledge of certain practical fundamentals, however, will be of service to the amateur.   He should know that tone in speech, as in singing, is made upon the vowels; that the quality is largely determined by the vowel color which predominates; that the average speaking voice will be improved by employing more of the "oo" or long "o" quality in the tone; that this tone should float or be sustained on an even flow of breath, and be characterized by the same absence of rigidity as that which exists in a perfect singing tone.

CONSONANTS

The young actor will also find it advantageous to cultivate deliberateness in speaking, particularly during the early rehearsals.   In the articulation of consonants, it is helpful for the pupil to keep in mind that these sounds serve to begin or to interrupt the tone—i. e., the vowel; the consonants therefore should not be prolonged, but on the contrary they should be crisp and distinct.   Final consonants require special attention; they must be articulated in a forward fashion with the tip of the tongue against the teeth or lips, so that each sound will be clearly audible—in contrast to the common habit of "swallowing" sounds like *d's*, *t's*, and *p's*.

It will be profitable to spend time upon the final word of each phrase; for children, as well as adults, very frequently employ a marked falling inflection, amounting to a sudden lowering of the pitch, on the closing words of a line or phrase.

"And what is so rare as a day *i*
n
Ju
ne?

Then, if ever, come perfect *d*
ay
s;

Then Heaven tried earth if it be *in*
tune,

And over it softly her warm
ear
lays.

The average person reads the first seven or eight syllables of each line quite distinctly; on the final word, however, the pitch of his voice suddenly drops and the last word is practically inaudible. The holding of rehearsals in the auditorium where the final performance is to be given will be helpful in securing good diction. It will be well to have some adult located in the rear of the auditorium, during rehearsals, to warn the director if the enunciation is poor and if the voices do not carry. Should the young actor fail to correct his inaudibility, the desired clearness and volume should be acquired through individual rehearsals.

Realizing, then, the importance of diction in the operetta, the director should see that each principal give careful attention to the diction in solos, and he should likewise be scrupulously exacting in regard to the diction of the spoken lines.

CUES

The few words of a speech, a measure or two of music, a

sound off stage, or possibly some particular bit of pantomime which comes just before a character enters, speaks, or exits, is called that character's "cue." Each principal must therefore memorize the two speeches, or it may be a measure or two of music, which directly precede his action or speech. The first speech is designated as the "warning" or "get ready" cue; the second, as the "entrance" cue; and they are so marked in the prompt copy. When an entrance follows directly upon the close of a song, the opening music of the song is the "entrance" cue. The young actor should be drilled from the beginning to be *ready* in the wings in order that following the "warning cue" his "entrance cue" may be taken instantly. The lack of insistence upon this point by the stage manager often retards the action during rehearsals,—the result being a slow tempo and a tedious final performance. If a tardy actor has to be hunted out from some place back-stage, he not only will be quite out of the spirit and character of his part, but, by his late entrance, he will destroy for his fellow actors; and for the audience as well, the realism of the scene. The stage manager should therefore remember that it is just as important for the actor to memorize cues as it is to memorize lines. When memorizing is insisted upon, there will be no hesitation in dialogue, and the tempo of the scene will be maintained. In an article entitled *Make Them Do It Well*, George Bernard Shaw says, "*Never have a moment of silence on the stage except as an emotional stage effect*. The play must not stop while an actor is getting up or sitting down or walking off the stage. He must sit on a word and rise on a word; if he has to make a movement he must move as he speaks, not before or after; and the cues must be picked up as smartly as a ball is fielded in cricket. This is the secret of holding an audience. It is a rule which you may set aside again and again to make a special effect; for a technical rule may always be broken on purpose but as a rule of thumb it is invaluable." Many an operetta is dull and lifeless because the actors make their movements in silence between the speeches—a situation easily avoided if cues are properly memorized and promptly taken.

PLAYING THE PART

Before an actor comes upon the stage he should think himself into his part, and having entered, he should remain in character until he has made his exit. So real to Sarah Bernhardt were all her characterizations that if spoken to off-stage during a performance, she invariably replied in the character she was playing. Not infrequently amateur performers, just as soon as their speeches are delivered, lapse

BALANCED GROUPINGS

(Actors "in character," and appropriately costumed)

into their own personalities; thus they destroy the illusion of the scene and are said to be "out of character."

THE COMEDY ROLE

Comedy parts overdone often distract attention from the person who should be the center of interest. Let the comedian display his talent and originality when his action is necessary to the story and during his own solos and speeches. Keep him in the background at other times. "Let those that play your clowns, speak no more than is set down for them." It should be remembered that one gesture belongs to the funny man and is his alone; when he wishes for any reason to indicate himself or emphasize his physical characteristics he employs his thumb to point with.

THE SUM TOTAL OF ACTING

George Bernard Shaw says that stage technique consists in making the audience believe that real things are happening to real people.

Shakespeare put into the mouth of Hamlet the simplest and the most adequate instructions that have ever been offered to the aspirant for dramatic fame, "Speak . . . trippingly on the tongue . . . do not saw the air too much with the hand, but use all gently . . . be not too tame neither . . . suit the action to the word, the word to the action . . . the purpose of playing is to hold, as 'twere, the mirror up to nature."

CHAPTER IX

Of equal importance with the choice and coaching of the principals is the selection and training of the chorus; for no degree of excellence on the part of the principals can compensate for mediocre work on the part of the chorus. The director should remember that this body of singers forms the background of the stage picture against which the principals sometimes stand out in relief; occasionally it constitutes almost the entire picture, as in opening scenes and in finales. The choice of chorus members should not, therefore, be the result of haphazard selection.

MEMBERSHIP

The chorus for the school operetta usually includes members of the glee-clubs and the large chorus. From whichever of these groups the singers are chosen, they should be carefully selected. They should be chosen on the basis of, first, voice quality and singing ability; second, personality; third, dependability; and fourth, freedom of bodily movement. It will also add to the versatility of the chorus if those in it have some knowledge of simple dance steps.

The chorus of an amateur production will in some measure be determined by local conditions; the members should, however, be selected with care.

SIZE OF GROUP

The size of the chorus will in some measure depend upon the physical condition of the stage, the number of singers available, and the demands of the operetta—that is, the

number of people who must or may be included in the production.   If the chorus is too large, it becomes unwieldy in
its action, it entails an increased expense for costumes, and
it makes more difficult the matter of attendance at and
management of rehearsals.   On the other hand, if it is too
small, it limits the training to a few persons, furnishes an
insufficient body of tone, and arouses the personal interest
of only a small number of people in the community.

REHEARSAL HINTS

Having early worked out a rehearsal schedule, the conductor will plan for each rehearsal so that it will accomplish
a maximum in the time allotted; to this end, the rehearsal
should begin on time, the work should be intensive throughout the period, and the practice should be brought to a
close promptly on time.   A prolonged practice usually fails
of desired results; for the interest of the members lags and
their effort becomes half-hearted.   The number of rehearsals
which are necessary for the adequate preparation of a
chorus depends somewhat upon the grade of the operetta
and the ability of those participating; proper management
on the part of the director, however, should in most cases
complete an operetta within a period ranging from six to
eight weeks.   The director will expedite the work of preparation if he sees to it that the earlier rehearsals are devoted
solely to singing and the rehearsals for action are begun
only after the music of several scenes has been practically
memorized.

MEMORIZING MUSIC

As has been suggested in a previous chapter, the most
satisfactory preparation will be secured by a carefully
worked out rehearsal schedule.   The supervisor will find
that the preparation of the chorus will be facilitated by
adopting a definite procedure instead of going aimlessly

through an unlimited series of repetitions of music and action. It goes without saying, that the first requisite for a good chorus is perfect memorization by each member. The conductor should see that an adequate number of copies of the operetta are secured; these, of course, should be paid for from the proceeds of the performance, unless members of the chorus wish to purchase their own copies in order to keep them as souvenirs of the occasion. Inexperienced or uninformed conductors sometimes make copies of the words or music of an operetta for use at chorus rehearsals. These persons are doubtless unaware that this procedure is not only unsatisfactory, but what is of greater moment, that it is highly unethical.

As a first step in memorizing, the conductor should at the opening rehearsal outline briefly the story of the operetta; similarly if he will make a statement of the events which lead up to a particular chorus and give a description of the setting in which it is sung, this will do much toward creating for the singers the desired atmosphere and toward arousing that ever important essential—interest. He should determine beforehand what choruses are to be memorized at each rehearsal, and work intensively toward the accomplishment of this end. The conductor should avoid going over more material than can be memorized at a single rehearsal. During the early rehearsals he should see to it that the singers fix their minds upon the words and give special attention to the matter of memorization. After a chorus of average length has been sung through as a whole he may have the chorus sing four or eight lines, then close their books and discover just how much they have learned. Silent study of the words for a moment or two is often an aid toward rapid memorizing. The conductor should note carefully those measures in which words are forgotten; he should also observe which singers are memorizing slowly, in order to give special attention to them. Observation of the individuals in a group is made easy when the singers are seated in a semicircle, an arrangement which enables the director to discover by means of his eyes as well as by his ears those who are making slow progress. The inexperienced conductor should learn that his chorus includes two types of singers; first, those who work intensively and memorize rapidly; second, those who memorize slowly and sometimes incorrectly. Occasionally he will find that there are a few who really make no effort and who expect the rehearsal to be pure entertainment. Obviously the elimination of this latter group will add to the efficiency of the entire chorus. The conductor should discover and give special attention to those who make up group two, for failure to do so will materially retard the progress of group one and the preparation of the chorus as a whole. Flagrant mistakes, sometimes leading to a catastrophe on the night of the performance, can be traced directly to those singers who have not done their part during the period of rehearsals.

The conductor should from the opening rehearsal give attention to errors in the music or in the words; for the mispronunciation of a word or the singing of a wrong interval repeatedly at several successive rehearsals may unexpectedly recur on the night of the final performance. In rehearsals that are primarily for memorization, a light tone properly supported should be employed (Cf. Chapter XI). A suggestion from the conductor as to the meaning of a particular phrase will give to an important word the emphasis that is often necessary to obtain a singing climax.

Effective singing rehearsals of the chorus, then, will be secured if the conductor insists upon intensive study of a limited amount of material, if he tests the process of memorizing by frequently laying aside the score and having the chorus sing without it, and if he observes closely the progress of the individual members as well as that of the group as a whole.

CHAPTER X

The Dramatic Action of the Chorus

When the curtain rises upon the opening scene, it is usually the chorus which strikes the key-note of the entire operetta. It is, therefore, essential that the chorus as a whole shall not only sing well but shall also act well; to this end each individual member should be well-trained, alert throughout the entire performance, and lend to the ensemble every atom of animation he possesses. A chorus which may have been taught to sing accurately and with spirit, may not appear at all to advantage on the stage because of the failure to combine appropriate dramatic action with the singing. A properly balanced production, therefore, requires that the stage manager through definite direction and repeated drill develop the chorus action to as high a point of perfection as that to which the conductor has developed the musical numbers.

WHEN TO BEGIN DRAMATIC ACTION

In his eagerness to get the dramatic phase of the operetta under way, the stage manager is often tempted to put the chorus on the stage much too early. A stage rehearsal at which action is attempted while some of the singers hold open scores in their hands is manifestly a waste of time; for only after the members of the chorus have memorized the music of an act or scene can they give their attention to the dramatic action. The first action given to the chorus should be that which occurs independently of the principals. When this has been fixed, the stage business in which both chorus and principals have a part should be learned. After

71

the principals and chorus are thoroughly familiar with their stage business, then, and then only should a general rehearsal for action be called.

GROUP ACTION

Frequently the stage manager allows the numerous other details of preparation to crowd out attention which should be given to group action. He then falls back upon the fallacious idea that young players, if given a suggestion, will enter into the spirit of a scene and assume their roles naturally. But unfortunately, experience disproves this idea.

UNDIRECTED ACTION

Not infrequently a grade operetta presents the following picture: The moment for the chorus entrance arrives. The off-stage throng is released. Lack of specific instructions at rehearsals causes them to hesitate, bewildered! A few of the more self-possessed young actors start forward, looking back as they go, to catch the hurried, "Quick, go on!" which has been whispered by a teacher in the wings. Some of the more impatient actors push, and, like a pent-up stream, the crowd finally surges across the stage to mass itself at a point determined by chance. At an impromptu signal from "someone," the mob distributes itself more or less unevenly across the stage, and the scene is on! The principals play their parts and at the close of the scene the self-conscious chorus, ill at ease, and quite unrelated to what has been going on, rushes off the stage,—that is, the leaders do; the less fortunate and slower members linger, and the exit drags itself out to the discomfiture of audience and chorus alike.

DIRECTED ACTION

Action for groups must be worked out in detail and rehearsed repeatedly in order to secure that precision, team work, and correlation of word and movement which characterize professional and good amateur choruses. At the first rehearsal for action the stage manager may well spend time in giving the chorus preliminary instruction in the fundamentals of stage deportment, such as posture, balance of groups, gesture of location, cues, entrances, and exits (Cf. Chapter viii). The various members will learn quickly by imitation and observation, and will thus avoid, to a large extent, the necessity for many corrections which might otherwise have to be made.

The chorus must necessarily follow the stage manger's directions very accurately and they should be given to understand that individual interpretation has no place in ensemble action, except as suggested or approved by the stage manager. For example, once in a while small groups, or even one person, may come out from the chorus for a bit of pantomime which has previously been worked out with the stage manager; the general effect of the chorus movement, however, should be that of concerted action. The stage manager should explain to the chorus that the action determined upon at the first rehearsal may be subsequently altered if a better effect can be obtained by such a change. Once the action is settled, however, it is absolutely necessary that each member of the chorus know definitely where he is to stand on the stage, and exactly what his action and pantomime are to be. During the early rehearsals, individuals who are known to have initiative must be watched in order that they may not interpolate their own ideas into the stage manager's picture (Cf. Chapter xvii).

UNIFORMITY OF ACTION

All chorus action that is supposed to be uniform and simultaneous can be made so only by painstaking and repeated drill. The stage manager should select the particular word in a phrase upon which word a given gesture is to be made; he should then drill the group on that gesture until the entire chorus does it in an identical manner and at the same time. When action takes place during an instrumental prelude or interlude, a certain chord should be designated as a cue for the specified gesture. Explicit directions given beforehand will economize time and effort: for instance, if the chorus is to kneel, every member must kneel at the same time, on the same chord, on the correct knee.* Or again, in a finale, the entire chorus may salute the returning victor. Upon a definite word or chord each person steps forward on his right foot, and on the next designated word or chord raises his right hand, extends his arm upward in perfect unison of action.

RELATING ACTION TO PRINCIPALS

Even though it remains up-stage or near the wings, the chorus should constantly reflect the action of the principals. This does not mean of course that a chorus must always be in motion; a smile or a frown, a movement of the head or a simple gesture is enough to relate the chorus work to that of the principals. When it is proper for the chorus to take the lead, as for example in driving off an offending character, cheering the hero, or protecting an innocent victim, the action should be definitely worked out.

DANCES

Whereas a director may, through the introduction of appropriate dances, add variety and interest to a children's or a primary operetta, the director of an intermediate grade or a junior high-school production should use dances

*When the chorus faces the audience directly, that is, when it forms a line across the stage from left to right, it is a matter of choice whether the right or left knee is used, providing the action is uniform; but in any other formation each person should kneel on the "down-stage" knee—the knee nearest the audience. If the chorus is arranged in diagonal lines, facing each other, the groups on the right, as the actor on the stage would view the audience, should kneel on the right knee, and the group on the left on the left knee.

sparingly. If, however, the stage picture be, for example, an Indian scene or a fair scene, a characteristic folk-dance may be employed to intensify the spirit of the scene. Unrelated dances, no matter how well executed, interrupt the continuity of any worth-while operetta. In practically every operetta, whether given by the high-school students or by amateurs in the community, there are various songs for the chorus or for small groups which may be made more effective by adding certain rhythmic movements, such as easy steps and appropriate gestures. The effect of dances or dance steps is determined not so much by their difficulty as by the finish with which they are performed. As in other phases of the preparation the director will, if he be wise, assign this part of the training to the instructor of physical education in the school, or a teacher of dancing in the community.

THE MISFITS

Inability of certain persons to appear well and to act in unison with the rest of the chorus may make it necessary to limit the action to a selected few, who should be placed in the front rows. For instance, a few persons who dance well can often put life and distinction into a chorus which, though it sings well, is limited in its dramatic action. Occasionally a member of the chorus who is awkward, or extremely tall, or otherwise conspicuous, finds an uncontrollable tendency to take a more prominent position on the stage than his person justifies; such a one should be very definitely located and specifically instructed as to his action. Or again, in a grade operetta, a nervous, active, or mischievous child may display some surprising mannerisms,—twisting a bit of his costume, relieving an imaginary mosquito bite, or disturbing the otherwise excellent stage demeanor of his associates; such action—most distracting at a public performance—should have been detected and checked at rehearsals.

CHORUS GROUPINGS

Under no circumstances should a chorus determine the grouping of its members.   The grouping must be made by the stage manager as he stands in front of the stage, where he can see the picture as a whole; and the first consideration should be such a distribution of the people on the stage as will produce a proper balance of individuals and of groups.

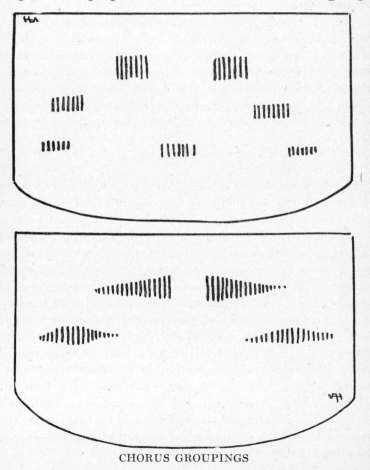

CHORUS GROUPINGS

When the chorus is arranged horizontally across the stage or in a semicircle formation, the tall people should be placed in the center, the shorter people next, and the shortest ones on each end.

When the large group is broken into several smaller groups, these smaller groups, each forming a picture by itself may be arranged in a variety of groupings. Individual groups may follow the arrangement of the large group in which the tall people are in the center; or the large group may be divided into small groups without any rearrangement as to height, the group in the center being made up of tall people, and those toward the wings, of shorter people. Again, the groups of short people may be placed down-stage near the audience and the tall ones located up-stage; whatever the arrangement, the stage manager and the actors themselves should make sure that the tall people do not hide the shorter ones from the view of the audience.

ENTRANCES

The playgoer who observes with any degree of keenness is aware that there is a great difference in the way in which actors come on the stage. The skillful manner in which a professional comes into a scene is not unlike the unobtrusive but definite entrance of a good conversationalist into a discussion. He does not come in tardily in a lumbering fashion, neither does he burst in abruptly;—just so with good entrances—when the movement of the play develops a situation in which the actor is required, he is there. Like other stage business the technique of entrances must be learned. In every good entrance however there are certain essentials.

PROMPTNESS

The first essential of a good chorus entrance is that it *must be on time*. A belated entrance causes embarrassment to those on the stage and delays the action. To insure correctly timed entrances, chorus groups must have leaders, —reliable people who possess self-confidence and dramatic sense, who pay attention to directions, and who remember details.   A good leader will take the responsibility for the entrances of his group.   When the entrance is military or formal he will get the members into position and in step ready to lead them, at the moment the cue is given, to the exact spot assigned on the stage.

QUICKNESS

A second requisite of a good chorus entrance is that it should consume no more time than is necessary.   In most amateur productions, the tempo or movement of an operetta is at a standstill during entrances and exits; entrances that are finished quickly therefore maintain the tempo of the production and hold the interest of the audience.   When the effect of a crowd is desired, the chorus may enter hastily through two or more entrances; and a quick movement of those first upon the stage away from the place of entrance and down stage will hasten the entrance of the remainder of the chorus.   A mass entrance is often intensified by the use of some "hurry up" measures from the musical score or a fanfare, as in the Finale of Act II of *The Mikado*.   On the other hand, it is sometimes necessary that a large group coming on the stage should appear to enter leisurely; in such a case the chorus should be separated into small groups and all available entrances used.

COMPLETENESS

A third essential of a good entrance is completeness.   An entrance is properly completed only when the players have arrived at their assigned positions on the stage in the most direct manner possible.   To accomplish this the stage manager will first have the actors "walk" their entrances in order that they may understand just where they are to enter and

the exact spot to which they are to go.   For example, in
Act I of *The Fire Prince*, by Henry Hadley, the King, who
is thoroughly out of temper with his son, has been stomping
back and forth across the stage down front.   The King
speaks, "I'll show him.   Hi!   Summon the Court.   I'll dis-
inherit him."   The King, having reached a position right
center in time to meet the principals who have just entered
from the right second entrance, exclaims, "Ah, here you
are."   Meanwhile the chorus enters: from the left third entrance come the groups composed of taller men and women
who stands up-stage; from the left second entrance at the
same time those of medium height; while from the first left
entrance come those of short stature, who will stand at the
left down front; such an entrance is both prompt and complete.

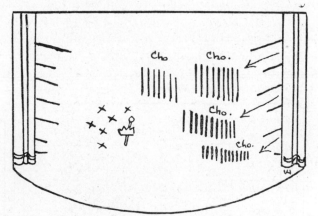

A PROMPT CHORUS ENTRANCE IN *THE FIRE PRINCE*

IN CHARACTER

A fourth essential of a good entrance is that it should
always be made "in character," that is, after the manner
and mood of the personalities assumed by the characters.
For illustration, a chorus represents a band of smugglers

stealing to their rendezvous. How would smugglers walk
—erect, straight ahead?—or sneaking along in the shadows,
listening for the dreaded guards, bending low under their
heavy burdens? One would probably stop suddenly, lest he
make a sound; another would turn back to signal his com-
panions that the way was clear, etc.

The essentials of good entrances which have been mentioned may be well illustrated in the entrance of the men's
chorus for "Behold The Lord High Executioner" in the well
known opera, *The Mikado*, by Gilbert and Sullivan. The
retainers are to enter in two lines, from opposite sides. At
the first measure of the introduction, the leaders on each
side, off-stage, whisper "left" on the first beat of the
measure, and every man quietly marks time, so that at the
given cue the leaders from the opposite wings simultaneously
lead out to the center-back. In a double line they march
well down to the foots, and with a right and left wheel form
a line across the stage. In preparation for Ko-Ko's entrance the two lines swing back, upon the "cue word," to a *V*
formation, or march to form two parallel lines extending
from the foots up-stage.

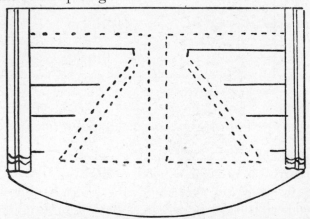

ENTRANCE OF RETAINERS IN *THE MIKADO*

ENTRANCES TO MUSIC

Frequently the entrance of a chorus is made much more effective if it is taken during the instrumental prelude. When it is to be so taken, the stage manager must discover the exact number of bars of the music which will be required to bring the singers on the stage and in position at the precise moment when they should begin singing. Should there be no prelude, the orchestra or the accompanist may play, in place of an introduction, a few measures of the song itself followed by a definite cadence. Again, interest is added to a chorus entrance when the scene and the music permit the chorus to sing as they enter; such an entrance, however, demands careful rehearsal to insure perfect attack, agreement in tempo, and uniformity of movement. The music used may be the refrain or the closing strain of the verse; occasionally the entire verse may be sung and then repeated as soon as the singers are in position on the stage.

MASSED AND SCATTERED ENTRANCES

Chorus entrances are of two general kinds—massed and scattered. The former type of entrance is illustrated by the mob, and almost without exception, such entrances are hastened by admonishing each player to "hurry." The scattered entrance is exemplified by a fair scene—so popular with librettists. Joyous groups of country girls and boys, farmers and their wives, peddlers offering their wares to fine ladies come on the stage from several entrances, some from one side, some from the other, some single, some in groups. Several saunter across the stage and make purchases. Another groups speaks in pantomime to friends. Others curtsey to the squire, and so on. This sort of stage business which was also illustrated in the smuggler's scene just referred to is highly valuable in that it lends naturalness, life, and local color to a scene. It should, however, be used merely as suggestive by-play—the background of a picture.

Unless the text denotes otherwise, all such action should be silent; moreover, like every other type of stage business, it should not be prolonged or exaggerated, as amateurs and occasionally professionals are sometimes tempted to do. This type of action is often referred to as "*ad lib.*"

EXITS

Exits have the same essentials and demand the same careful preparation as do entrances. Too often the amateur drops out of character before he drops out of sight. The stage manager must adapt the details of the exit to the tempo of the scene. Some exits must be taken hastily, others slowly. Singing and dancing exits are effective in an operetta. For these special music is sometimes written in the score. If, however, such special music is not provided, it is legitimate for the stage manager to adapt whatever bits of the music score he finds suitable for simple dance steps to be used for exits or entrances, as well as for interludes between the verses of the songs. At times an exit is made on the last phrase of the song; again, it may be necessary to repeat a phrase or more of the music in order that the exit may not appear hurried. The stage manager should see to it that the faces of the chorus are turned well toward the audience, particularly when spoken or singing lines are given during the exit.

HURRIED EXITS

Hurried exits are often necessary for carrying out the spirit of a scene. In *The Prince of Martinique*, by Stoughton, the Prince offers a hundred gold ducats to the man who will bring from the harbor the captain of the vessel which has just been sighted. The crowd rushes off to the right through the trees. If there are two woodwings, these will afford three exits toward which three leaders may start immediately upon the announcement of the Prince; their groups should go with them, some pushing their way through the crowd, others gesticulating excitedly to those nearest to them, one perhaps falling down in his haste, another beckoning to his friend to hurry that they may at least see the strange ship—all, however, particularly those who are last to leave, holding the spirit of the exit until they are off the stage.

LEISURELY EXITS

An exit of quite a different sort occurs after the Prince, who has promised ten louis to each, withdraws into the palace. Singing "Long live the Prince," the chorus leaves the stage, again right, this time, however, in an unhurried fashion. Some of them look back upon the palace, waving their hands; some nod their heads approvingly; others count, in anticipation, the promised money, their faces turned more often toward the audience than away; and the last few of the crowd, all in earnest conversation, saunter off, arm in arm.

MAINTAINING THE MOOD

Every exit, as well as every entrance, should be stamped with some very positive quality which the chorus action should not fail to express. Not only should each actor hold his individual character, but he should also keep the general mood of the scene until he is beyond the wings. If preceding the exit there is singing or animated conversation which is supposed to continue off-stage, the voices should, in order to give the effect of distance, gradually soften until they finally die away. This effect of receding voices will be heightened if the chorus, or part of it, continuing to sing, enters a nearby room, the door of which is then slowly closed. During rehearsals, exits and entrances should be practiced frequently in order that their special character may be emphasized and the action made smooth.

LEADERS

In good exits, as in good entrances, capable leaders are invaluable. Such leaders should be letter-perfect in their cues for action and alert to begin the exit on time and in the spirit which the scene demands. When required, these leaders should move some of the chorus in anticipation of the exit so that it will be natural rather than an exit of a few followed by many leaving the stage in the manner of a procession. Some of them will make the exit more effective if they remain until the last, finishing the exit in character.

FINALES AND CURTAIN CALLS

In the course of stage rehearsals the actors should become familiar with the action which is called for at the close of scenes. During the finale and when they are taking curtain calls there is a tendency on the part of large groups, and sometimes on the part of the principals, to "let down"—to become themselves. All persons on the stage should remain in character, otherwise the scene will simply be a stilted photograph. The first curtain call is a tableau, an exact duplicate of the scene upon which the last curtain fell. If a second curtain call is taken, acknowledgment of applause is made as follows: the members of the cast bow first to the audience and then to each other, the chorus maintains the atmosphere of the scene and a quick curtain follows. At the dress rehearsal, or the rehearsal preceding it, the man in charge of the curtain should practice raising and lowering it in accordance with carefully determined cues and at the speed demanded by the scene, for a scene full of sentiment will frequently be heightened in effect by a slowly lowered curtain, whereas a tense moment at the close of an act will be accentuated by a quick curtain.

To make the chorus life-like every moment that it is on the stage should be the aim of the stage manager. Toward this end he should drill his chorus on cues, entrances, exits,

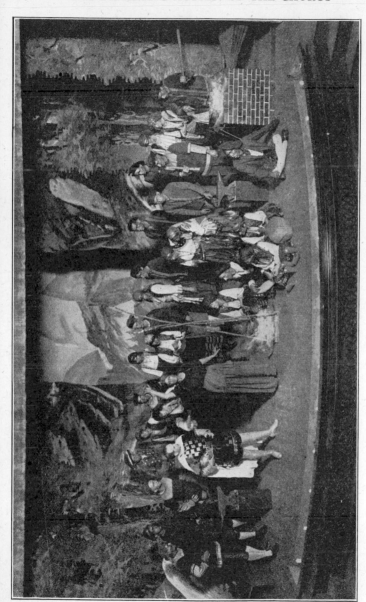

IL TROVATORE
(The first curtain call)

and curtain calls, trying to remove from the stage business as much artificiality as possible and to infuse into the performance just as much spontaneity and naturalness as the members are capable of developing.

CHAPTER XI

Making the Music Effective

Realizing that the character of the entire production is determined by the quality of the several details that go to make up the operetta, the director will naturally endeavor to give adequate attention to all of them. Since he is confronted, however, by the demands of scenery, lighting, or other phases of the preparation with which he may be unfamiliar, he may be tempted to assume that the musical ends of the production will be attained if a sufficient number of rehearsals bring about a perfect memorization of the music. This, however, is not sufficient. The music to be effective must, first of all, be sung intelligently; for as each bit of dialogue adds something to the story, so the several solos and choruses aid in the unfolding of the plot. In addition, the music of the operetta must satisfy the ear—it must be pleasing as to quality, intonation, balance of parts, and diction.

SINGING TONE

A prime requisite which is often overlooked in the presentation of an operetta is that of a singing tone which is both adequate and satisfying. The conductor should not for a moment forget that tone is the vehicle through which the musical message is carried. If, then, the quality is forced, or unsupported, the general character of the production will be far below the standard which would have been attained if the vocal tone had been rich and full, satisfactory in intonation, and suited alike in carrying power to both broad and fine effects.

Whereas the operetta on the one hand may furnish an

unusual incentive for singing, it is quite possible for the conductor so to ignore the vocal limitations of his singers that the musical effect of the operetta is seriously impaired and the voices temporarily injured. Notwithstanding the fact that the average conductor is familiar with the fundamentals of good tone, unless he is constantly alert, he may fail to give these fundamentals attention.

Although a comprehensive discussion of the subject of voice production is here neither pertinent nor possible, a brief consideration of some of the vocal details which the conductor should keep in mind may not be amiss.

TUNING THE CHORUS

At the beginning of a rehearsal the singers may be put into condition for good tune and tone through the use of a loose sustained hum which sounds on the lips and is held through sixteen or more seconds. This exercise will also be helpful in the middle of a rehearsal when voices seem tired or deficient in intonation. The average supervisor and vocal conductor *talks* much of tone quality; he will best *prove* his creed by the tonal character of his vocal groups. "But," objects the anxious director, "this vocal drill will take precious time from rehearsals which are altogether too brief." On the contrary, experience will prove that more and better work will be accomplished if a brief tuning up period precedes the rehearsal. If done in an intensive manner such preparatory "tuning up" need not occupy more than two or three minutes; the result will justify the time expended.*

CONSERVING VOICES

The conductor in his effort to secure a dramatic result at a given rehearsal, is often tempted to allow his singers to

Tuning-up Exercises by H. C. Maybee, published separately for women's, men's, and mixed voices, and for junior high school (Oliver Ditson Co.) will be of great help for this purpose.

produce a tone that is forced in quality. He should realize that full voice effects are not essential at the average rehearsal, though they may be required for certain numbers at the public performance. Not infrequently a conductor overlooks the opportunities afforded by certain chorus or solo numbers for a lovely pianissimo passage; these spots with their fine shading and nuance are not only impressive in themselves but they afford excellent contrast to the fortissimo passages which are of frequent occurrence. Again, the conductor should not lose sight of the value of this lighter type of singing in its toning up and sometimes tuning up the voices themselves.

BALANCE OF PARTS

Nor will the alert conductor overlook the matter of balance of parts. Although the dramatic demands of the production may require an equal number of men's and women's voices, he should see to it that the sopranos are not overburdened with the effort to produce a volume equal to that of the tenors and basses; obviously the remedy for this type of unbalanced tone is to reduce the volume of the men's voices. Often the relative number of men's and women's voices is determined by the director, and he should therefore include more women's voices than men's.

In a children's operetta where the number of persons in a scene is limited by the size of the stage or by the dramatic action, a supplementary chorus concealed in the wings will add volume, strengthen a weak part, and include a larger number in the production.

INTONATION

Not infrequently, poor intonation seriously detracts from the otherwise excellent work of a chorus or soloist. Too often faulty pitch is due to lack of attention to the matter at early rehearsals, both on the part of the conductor and on the part of the singers. It is often traceable to one or two individual voices. These individuals may not always be out of tune, but in certain places in the music they may be consistently off pitch. If after individual attention the singer is unable to remedy the fault, a simple expedient is for the director to tell this singer to be quiet during the singing of certain bars, whispering the words but making no sound. Such an arrangement, of course, should be known only to the conductor and the singer involved. Rigidity, especially tenseness of the jaw, tongue, and throat muscles, is often the cause of incorrect intonation. An observant conductor or a vocal teacher may frequently correct this condition in a singer by giving individual attention to his case. To illustrate, the baritone lead in a certain operetta was always faulty in the matter of pitch; the first verse of his solo was flat and the second still more so. This incorrect pitch might have been ignored had it not been for the fact that the chorus which took up the finale was unable to sing in a tone approaching anything like correct pitch. An individual rehearsal with the baritone revealed the fact that on a peculiar word he crowded his tongue to the back of his mouth, set his jaw, and attempted a high head tone. A few suggestions and a half hour's practice before a mirror temporarily remedied the difficulty. In order to improve the intonation, the conductor should aim to keep before his singers the thought of correct pitch, the importance of securing *natural* vowel sounds, and of obtaining active but unforced breathing.

CHILDREN'S VOICES

A comment regarding primary and lower grade operettas may here be pertinent. In these productions the tone quality is usually unforced and often negatively good, but the tone and the words are heard with difficulty. As a rule this tone may be made positively good if the director will secure, indirectly of course, good posture and a connection between tone and breath. The former is commonly brought about by the simple correction of what is known as the "fatigue" position caused by slumping shoulders and a too relaxed or protruding abdominal wall; the latter—connection between tone and breath—may be secured through the singing of a sustained and steady tone and the taking of breath at less frequent intervals. A neglect of either of these essentials just mentioned will result in a vocal tone that will be quite inadequate. If, however, a conductor is unable safely to add power to children's voices, a light unforced tone is always preferable to that strident quality which is sure to result from the single injunction, "Sing good and loud!"

In staging primary operettas, if the school auditorium is too small to accommodate the audience in a single performance, it will be better to give two performances in the small room than to employ a large auditorium in which the children's voices will be forced and strained, or the audience be disappointed because of inaudibility.

THE ACCOMPANIST

In the preparation of the operetta the importance of an efficient accompanist cannot be overemphasized. The conductor should choose a person who has sufficient time to devote to all solo, chorus, and general rehearsals. A solo pianist who cannot follow will be of less service than a willing accompanist of only average ability who will spend all the time that is necessary to perfect her work. She should become so familiar with the music that she can watch the conductor freely and occasionally the singers when necessary. From the beginning it should be understood that the baton and not the piano will lead. This fact may be brought forcibly to the attention of all by the conductor's early insistence upon attacks, holds, and changes of tempo. An assistant accompanist, preferably a member of the chorus, is an absolute necessity.

THE ORCHESTRA

A small orchestra carefully trained in the music and in the matter of subordinating the accompaniment will increase the musical value and attractiveness of the production. The players should be good readers and above all should play absolutely in tune; the wind instruments, especially the brass, should be watched in this latter particular. The conductor should hold orchestra rehearsals separately from those of the chorus in order that the various parts may be carefully worked out and the tempo and shading established. Futhermore, it should be thoroughly understood that the orchestra is to be, primarily, an accompaniment. If an orchestra is not sufficiently dependable and experienced to play the entire score, it may, perhaps, be used for the introduction and interludes. For light solo voices the piano and violin are often preferable to a large instrumentation. Here again a kindly critic at rehearsals will be of service in helping to determine what accompaniment will be best suited to the different voices. The violin will be found to be an aid in the matter of pitch stability, the mute being used if a very soft accompaniment is desired. Occasionally a violin played behind the scenes will help a large chorus to maintain pitch and rhythm. When the orchestra is to be used for the entire score, combined rehearsals with the chorus should not be held until both groups are thoroughly familiar with their parts. However, they should practice together at least once before the dress rehearsal.

To make the operetta most effective musically, the quality of vocal tone must never be lost sight of. The conductor will do well to keep in mind the fact that the average operetta will be given but once; the voices of the singers will be used for years to come. No vocal effect therefore will justify the misuse of the voices of the cast and chorus. Futhermore, the director in his choice of the operetta should remember that a work which has no moments that are really musical—from a vocal standpoint—is unworthy of the time of the conductor, the cast, or the chorus.

CHAPTER XII

The Scenery

Scenery from the Chinese point of view is as real as the observer cares to imagine it. Many operettas, however, make an impossible demand upon the imagination. The repeated use of the same old settings means a distinct loss in artistic effect, for attractive music or picturesque costumes cannot convert a scarred interior into a Japanese garden full of blooming cherry trees. Moreover, since the spirit with which the cast and chorus enter into a scene is materially affected not only by the costumes, but also by the stage setting itself, it is most necessary that adequate attention be given to this part of the preparation for the operetta.

STAGE TERMINOLOGY

In his preparation for staging an operetta, the supervisor, or amateur director, will see and hear terms with which he may be unfamiliar. Since these terms are commonly employed in connection with the stage, the director should know them.

The *proscenium arch* is the opening through which the audience looks upon the stage. It forms the frame of the stage picture.

The *apron* is that portion of the stage, usually semicircular in form, which extends in front of the curtain.

Above the stage is the *gridiron*, an open framework, from which are suspended the main curtain and all hanging scenery, such as the borders and drops. These pieces are usually raised and lowered to the floor of the stage by means of ropes and pulleys, technically known as *lines* and *sheaves*. The sheaves, of which there are two or three for each scenic drop, are nailed to the gridiron; they consist of two wooden blocks between which is fastened an iron pulley, over which runs a rope, technically known as a line. One end of each line is tied into a hole of the wooden battens, or strips, to

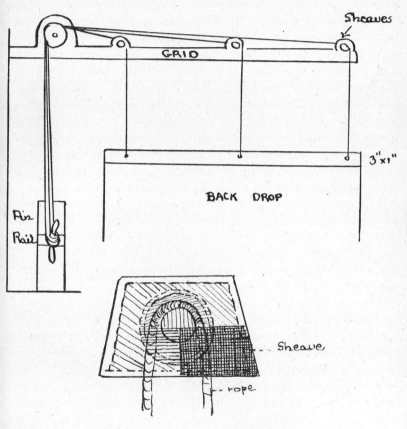

Sheaves

GRID

3"x1"

BACK DROP

Pin Rail

Sheave

rope

which the upper edge of the scenery is fastened; the other end of the line is tied to what is known as a pin block, a heavy beam in which holes are bored and which is usually located in a narrow, elevated platform on one side of the stage called the *fly gallery*. In case there is no fly gallery, the lines which serve to hold the weight of the scenery are tied to pegs or hooks in the side wall. Heavy pieces of scenery are handled more easily through the use of counter-weights attached to the outer end of the line holding the scenery. When the space above the proscenium arch is so limited as to preclude a gridiron, heavy screw eyes fastened to the transverse beams of the stage ceiling serve to hold the sheaves or pulleys through which the scenery lines pass.

The *tormentors*, two in number, are flat pieces built in two-part sections and hinged like a portable folding house-hold screen. The canvas with which they are covered is painted to give the effect of a draped-back curtain. These pieces are practically permanent, and are set at an obtuse angle on each extreme side of the proscenium arch and be-tween it and the next piece of scenery, so as to conceal the off-stage from the view of the audience.

The *grand drapery*, or *valance*, is a curtain of velour, or painted canvas, extending from three to five feet below the top of the proscenium arch. It serves, with the tormentors, as a permanent trim for the proscenium arch, hides the ceil-ing of the stage from the view of the audience, and conceals the front curtain when it is fully raised.

Flats are oblong frames, usually made of 1 x 3 lumber, 12 to 16 feet in height and 5′ 9″ in width; the corners of the frames are mitered and made solid by corrugated iron fasteners technically known as corrugators. Across these frames is stretched canvas or muslin; this material is first tacked along the inside edges of the frame, and is then glued to the frame. When the glue is set, the tacks are removed and the canvas, having been given a priming coat, is painted. Flats standing on end are placed edge to edge and lashed together by means of cleats and ropes. They are made firm by floor braces, the ends of which are hooked into screw eyes, one of the screw eyes being fastened into the frame and the other into the floor.

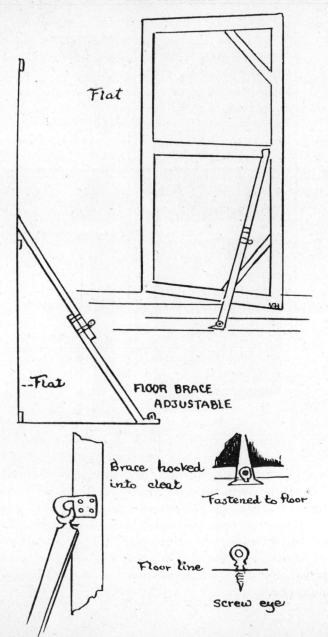

Flat

Flat

--Flat

FLOOR BRACE
ADJUSTABLE

Brace hooked
into cleat

Fastened to floor

Floor line

Screw eye

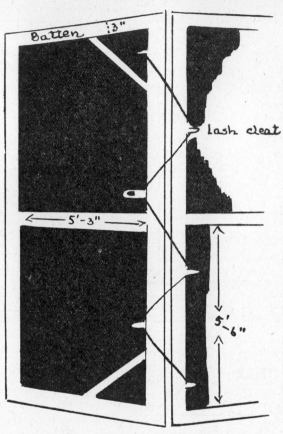

FLATS LASHED

The *Wings*, which, in their screen-like construction are similar to the tormentors, stand on end and are self supporting. Located on the sides of the stage, they represent trees or other exterior scenes which are suggested in the backdrops with which they are used. They are set in pairs on the stage, and furnish entrances which are numbered: "first entrance," "second entrance," and "third entrance," numbering from the front of the stage.

Borders are hangings which are suspended from the gridiron above at such a height as to obscure the view of the stage loft.   They are made to match the sets with which they are used—the wood set or the interior set—or else they are painted a plain blue to suggest the ceiling or sky.

Backdrops are single pieces of painted canvas, or lighter material, which are usually hung at the back of the stage. These drops are fastened at the top and bottom to battens. A batten, equal in length to the backdrop, is made of 1 x 3 pieces between which the canvas is held firmly by screws. Holes are bored through the top of the battens, and in these are tied the lines by which the drop is raised and lowered. The back drops are most commonly wood drops, marine views, and street scenes.

A *cut drop* is a canvas in which an archway is cut; it is hung in front of a backdrop which is painted to represent a far distant scene, of which the cut drop forms the foreground.   For illustration: the scene requires a rocky pass; the backdrop pictures the sky and mountains in the far distance; the cut drop, representing large rocks and trees in the near scene, is hung a few feet in front.   The actors may now appear to pass into the mountains to the right or left, after which they disappear behind the rocks of the cut drop.   By the use of an incline placed back of the cut drop and hidden by a masker, the actors will appear to climb upward into a mountain pass.

A *masker* is a low piece of flat scenery, such as a wall or hedge, which is placed in front of the bottom of a cut drop or elsewhere on the stage where it is necessary to conceal some stage device from the view of the audience, as has just been explained in the preceding paragraph.

A *street drop*, or a garden drop, is one which is often hung near the front curtain to make a shallow stage; in front of this drop the action of one scene may take place while the stage behind it is being set for the next act.

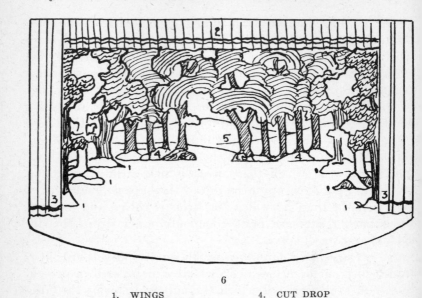

6

1.	WINGS	4.	CUT DROP
2.	VALANCE	5.	BACKDROP
3.	TORMENTORS	6.	APRON

PAINTED SCENERY

If the auditorium in which the operetta is to be given is equipped with the customary painted scenery, the director will have the choice of contructing new scenery or of revamping old sets. Whatever plans are determined upon, the supervisor or director should under no circumstances assume the responsibility for the scenery. A scenery committee, which will include the stage carpenter and the best talent from the art and manual training departments of the school, should have full charge of the scenery and should be given credit on the program for their work. This committee should be chosen early and should be allowed a sufficient amount from the budget with which to make the necessary purchases. They will go over the various scenes carefully with the director, draw the scene plots, and divide among themselves the responsibility of carrying out the plans. If no one of the art department is available, some individual in the community may be found whose avocation is some form of drawing or painting and who will be glad to assist the committee. The local sign painter may be of assistance, providing he can be made to understand that his work is to be impressionistic rather than realistic. The artist of the committee should make sketches and suggest suitable colors for particular scenes. Under the committee's supervision, skillful students can assist by constructing scenery that will give a professional stamp to the production. In one small city, a rector of a church, cooperating with members of the boys' glee club who were manually clever, built and painted the scenery for several operettas. Not only were new and attractive sets of scenery produced, but worth-while contacts were provided, both for the boys and for the minister. Not infrequently some unusually fine scenes have been produced by amateur scenic artists. Such pieces of scenery should be added to the stage equipment of the school.

CONSTRUCTING A BACKDROP

To construct the frame on which the backdrop is to be painted, 1 x 3 lumber should be used. If the uprights are made of 2 x 4's, the frame will be more stable. Next, canvas or muslin should be cut into lengths the desired height of the backdrop. These lengths should then be stitched together with the raw seam on the back side. The muslin tacked at the top and bottom should not be stretched tight, since the priming coat will cause it to shrink. Medium weight canvas forty inches wide, which sells for forty-five cents a yard, may be used; but unbleached muslin, though lighter in weight than canvas, will answer the purpose and will cost only ten or fifteen cents a yard.

Prime is the mixture employed for the first coat which must be used on all new materials before they can be painted. This prime consists of size, which is dissolved glue mixed with whiting; whiting costs ten cents per pound, and glue twenty cents. Size is made by dissolving ground glue in water and adding to this mixture whiting or grey ochre. Whiting thickens the mixture until it is of the consistency of thin paint, and heating causes it to dissolve. One pound of glue will make two gallons of size, and this amount will cover two hundred and fifty square feet of material. Three gallons of size will cover a backdrop 16 x 24. One coating of this prime fills the muslin, gives it body, and prepares it for the paint.

MAKING THE SKETCH

The artist member of the committee should first make a rough sketch on paper of the scene to be painted. This should be done in a broad way and lined off in squares to correspond to squares or rectangles which will be drawn later on the canvas. The predominating color forming the background—the gray of a wall, the green of a forest, or the blue of the sky—should first be painted on the previously-sized canvas or muslin. Although the canvas to be painted is often laid flat on the floor, a more practical plan is to support the material vertically against a wall. A bridge or movable platform will then be found to be more serviceable than stepladders, because such a device makes it possible for several people to work at the same time, and it also enables one individual to reach all parts of the canvas with ease. In reproducing the sketch on the canvas the first step is to strike at the bottom of the drop a base line which is to be used for measurements; four inches from the top another line should be struck off which will serve as a guide for the battens to which the drop will later be fastened for permanent use. Arcs drawn from each end of the base line will intersect at a point just above the mid-point of the base line. This base line and a line drawn from the intersection perpendicular to the base line, will serve as guide lines from which the entire surface may be lined off into squares. The perspective point will be on a level with the eye, about five and one-half feet above the base line. Except in a street

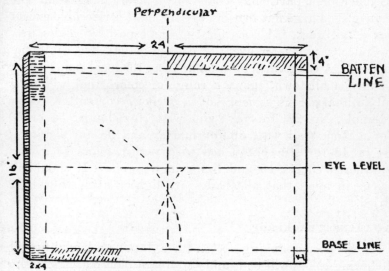

FRAMEWORK FOR PAINTING A BACKDROP

scene or in a broad landscape, the perspective may be ignored in painting the backdrop. The sketch which has been drawn to a relative scale should now be transferred with charcoal or chalk to the canvas.

PAINTING THE BACKDROP

Under the direction of the artist in charge, the assistants will block in the different sections, and when all of the sections are roughly completed the artist will fill in the details.

The materials used for scene painting are dry colors, purchasable by the pound at any hardware store. Paints which are known as "distemper colors," or Alabastine, are most practical. These paints should be mixed in water to which a small quantity of size has been added.   Pails will be needed for those paints which will be used in quantities—such as a blue and green.   Good-sized tin cups will hold as much of a particular color as the average amateur can manage.   Large flat brushes are the most serviceable except for detail work.   Alabastine tints and positive colors may be purchased at an average cost of thirty-five cents per pound.   A color card, obtainable from the local paint dealer of any small town, shows a range of colors that will meet all ordinary requirements of a scenery committee.   For example, No. 28, for sky; zinc white for clouds; 54 or 29 for a stone wall with 58 for mortar and 98 for shadows; 64 or 48 for stucco touched with varied colors to give a weathered effect; 15 and 6 for high lights.   It should be borne in mind that all shades are lighter after they have dried.

A JAPANESE BACKDROP

In the accompanying sketch for a Japanese backdrop the following colors will be found suitable: Color No. 2, shading to No. 28 at the right, in sections L-R, 1-5; for the rushes in the foreground and the pines, No. 5; for the other trees, brown trunks and a warmer green than that used for pines, —No. 16; No. 8 and No. 21 for the flowers; the pagoda and torii No. 58; for the brown of the pines and for the branches No. 97; for the bridge and lantern at E-11, No. 29; for the foreground of the picture No. 33 with lavender Nos. 28 and 21; for the trees at E-G, 7-8-9, No. 49; purple, Nos. 8 and 9, for the deep shadow of the bridge; for the path L-M-N-O, 8-9-10, No. 64 with lavender for shadows of the steps; for the mountains and volcano, a green with lavender for distance, and bluish white for the smoke of the volcano.

Amateur scenic painters should bear in mind that "distance lends enchantment" and that their work is merely to

A JAPANESE BACKDROP

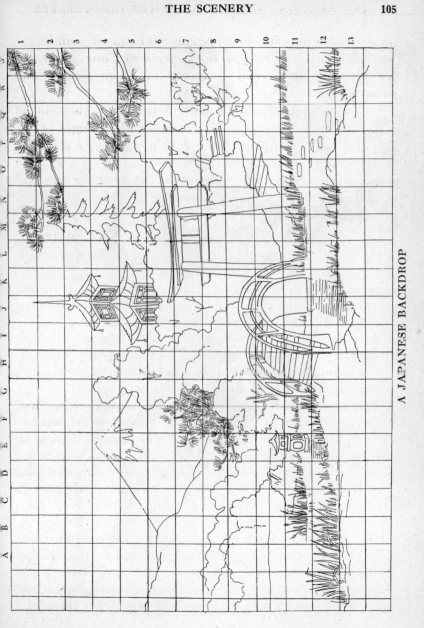

A JAPANESE BACKDROP

suggest—not actually to represent.   The novice will be encouraged in his efforts if he inspects at close range the
sketchy lines and broad treatment of stage scenery and
painted signs.

If wings are painted as a part of the scene, they should
carry out the ideas suggested at the extreme edges of the
backdrop; for example, the wings to be used with a marine
backdrop may represent a stretch of sand and rocks.   Most
commonly the wings are "woodwings" in keeping with the
wood backdrop.

REVAMPING OLD SCENES

Old scenery may be so altered as to create effective stage
pictures that are new.   A familiar interior, with slight expense but some labor, may be temporarily covered, bordered,
or wainscoted with plain paper or with wall paper fastened
to it with thumb tacks or paste.   Draperies may be substituted for doors.   A door may be made into a window or
a fireplace.   A coat of grey or green paint will make the
reverse side of a parlor set into a good kitchen or woodsman's
cabin.   If the walls of an old interior are laid off in rough
squares to represent stones, an archway built over the door
and wooden strips nailed across the window, the set becomes
a prison exterior.   Again, when three of four sections of an
interior scene are given a bluish grey background on which
large squares are outlined in black, the result is an attractive
Japanese interior.   When the reverse side of an interior
scene is painted blue, and a plate rail and a large two-section
cupboard door are added, the resulting interior easily suggests the home of a Dutch fisherman.   The familiar door
of an exterior set may be materially changed by the addition
of an overhanging roof with supporting posts and a small
platform.   An interior is remade when a newel post, a rail,
and a low flight of steps leading off stage from the center

SUGGESTIONS FOR BACKDROPS

SUGGESTIONS FOR BACKDROPS

back are added. An old interior, when it is painted grey, lined off into black or brown stones, embellished with vines and given a thatched roof entrance, will meet the requirements of an exterior of a Scotch or Irish scene. A small Kansas community, limited as to the size and scenic equipment of its stage was blessed with a committee which had sufficient ambition, initiative, and skill to paint on the back wall of the auditorium a creditable reproduction of a Jacob Van Ruysdael painting as the backdrop for an operetta

A "WALL" BACKDROP

(A scene painted on the rear wall of a shallow stage)

requiring a Dutch setting. Many similar ideas will suggest themselves to any one who has let himself catch the spirit of revamping old scenes.

SCENE SHIFTING

When the scenery in the stage setting is made up of the customary interiors, woodwings, and other painted scenery, the problem of scene shifting demands special consideration on the part of the stage manager. In stage parlance, to "strike a set" is to remove it from the stage. To have this done without delay and to have the following scene set up with promptness is the aim of every director as well as the ardent and sometimes vociferously expressed desire of the audience. To expedite a quick shifting of scenes, the stage manager should see to it that no one be allowed on the stage between acts except the stage carpenter and crew, the property man, and his assistants. Although the stage help may be familiar in a general way with their duties, only by practice can they develop that technique which will hasten their part of the rehearsal. If the stage manager is wise, he will assign to each stage hand definite tasks—the removal or replacement of special parts of the scenery, the change of certain properties, etc. At some of the early rehearsals devoted to stage setting alone, the director may use as an incentive for acquiring rapid shifts, a definite time limit within which the used setting is to be removed and the next one set up. Dress rehearsals often drag late into the night simply because the stage manager has neglected to have separate rehearsals for scenery and lighting.

A WINDOW STAGE

A novel arrangement for a small stage and cast or for a review is produced as follows: A huge window frame 8 x 10 or 12 x 16, according to the size of the stage, is placed on the front edge of a platform large enough to accommodate the actors in the several scenes. This platform should be at least ten inches above the floor. On all sides of the frame are curtains of a neutral color, preferably gray, tan, or black. At the back of the platform is hung a blue drop. With the house lights turned on, the actors take their places on the darkened stage. The house is then darkened; floodlights make the scene visible to the audience as through a window. The illusion of a window is heightened if a netting or gauze is hung just inside the frame. The stage settings and properties should be proportioned to the stage. This arrangement makes an excellent setting for tableaux at Christmas time or for other special occasions.

A WINDOW STAGE

SIMPLIFIED SCENERY

In contrast to the somewhat ornate and highly realistic scenery of the professional theater there has developed, in recent years, a marked simplification in stage setting. In this simplified setting—a change for which the Little Theater movement is largely responsible—screens, hangings, and curtain effects are employed in the place of customary painted scenery.

The *cyclorama*, commonly called a "cyc," whcih was originally of permanent plaster or concrete construction, is now a popular and inexpensive stage setting consisting of a continuous semicircular curtain or of several curtains so hung as to produce a continuous effect. It is neutral in color, frequently light blue, and extends from one side of the proscenium arch around the stage to the other side of the proscenium arch. A cyclorama creates the illusion of

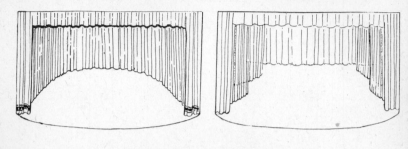

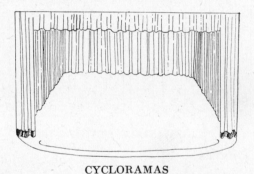

CYCLORAMAS

greater distance, and is susceptible of numerous and unusual lighting effects. Furthermore, with simple stage properties it may be used for a wide variety of settings.

Cycloramas are constructed of various materials: Monk's cloth is most commonly employed; burlap is less expensive but does not hang so well; black velvet makes a most effective cyclorama, but is costly; rep, thirty-six inches wide, costing eighty cents a yard; denim, thirty-six inches wide, costing sixty cents; sateen, twenty-seven inches wide, costing thirty-five cents; outing flannel, thirty-six inches wide, and priced at twenty cents;—all are serviceable materials for

cycloramas.   Blue cambric or dyed muslin will also be found
to be practical.

PINAFORE

(Cyclorama with practical entrances in the rear at R.U.E. and L.U.E.)

MAKING A "CYC"

To the upper end of the material, strips or upholsterer's
web should be stitched, to which strips the ropes or rings will
be fastened.   From an upholsterer, an awning-maker, or an
automobile repair man may be secured grommets—two-part
rings to be fastened through buttonholes in the web.   The
bottom of the curtain should be turned up and stitched so
as to make a pocket in which a chain or some other weight
can be placed for the purpose of making the curtain hang
evenly.   The curtains are usually hung from three battens
which are supported at the proper height by means of lines.
On a stage where there is no space overhead, the battens

may be screwed to the ceiling.   Although presenting an un-
broken effect, the cyclorama is so contructed that there are
three possible openings: one at the center back, and one on
each side.   At these openings the folds of the curtain, which
should be made with at least one-third to one-half fullness,

CYCLORAMA SETTING
(Cut-out trees, practical house and wall.   Note detail at left of picture)

overlaps two feet or more.   If the widths of material forming the curtain are not stitched together, doorways and
windows may be made wherever desired, and additional entrances may be provided for exteriors.   Two, or at the most
three borders should be hung to hide the stage ceiling; and
a backing of the same material as the cyclorama should be
set or hung back of the openings which are used for entrances and exits in order to conceal an off-stage view from
the audience.

The cyclorama is used for both exterior and interior stage
settings.   Motifs suggestive of the central idea of the
setting may be appliqued on the back and side curtains:
tulips and arms of windmills for a Holland scene; bows,

arrows, and tommyhawks for an Indian scene; dragons and Chinese posters for an oriental interior. Painted flat pieces cut from compo-board, as for example, columns, a fireplace, or a tree, add to the effectiveness of the setting.

SCREENS FOR SMALL STAGES

When stage space and funds for equipment are alike limited, the director will find screens to be both serviceable and inexpensive. The frames should be built and hinged in a fashion similar to that of the household screen, but they should be of larger dimensions. They may be six or eight feet high, depending upon the height of the stage opening; the sections, of which there may be two or three, should be thirty to forty-two inches wide. Muslin, after it has been primed and given two coats of a neutral gray into which some blue has been mixed, should be tacked on the frame. Burlap, which may be secured in a variety of shades, will also be found to make a durable and satisfactory covering for a set of screens. To obtain a harmonious effect at the back, the wall of the stage should then be painted to match. With four, or better, six, such screens and a back wall of a harmonizing color, a most serviceable stage setting can be provided at a smaller cost. This scenery may be used for interiors and exteriors. Conventional designs cut from colored paper and pasted or fastened on the screens and back wall will aid in creating the desired atmosphere; for instance, fleurs-de-lis will suggest a French scene, stars and a crescent moon a night picture, vines and branches a forest, and sprays of flowers a garden. Columns, arches, and set pieces from compo-board will give an added realistic touch to the setting, and the combined result will be far more artistic and flexible than the effect created by the battered, scar-covered painted scenes which may have been in use for years. By using the screens as has just been suggested, but by substituting for the painted wall a backdrop which is painted to match the screens and which may be hung about eighteen inches in front of the back wall, there will be provided a passageway across the stage through which the actors and the different people on the stage may cross during a scene, unobserved by the audience. Again, in those rural and community high schools in which the doors leading off from the sides of the stage open directly into the main auditorium, screens may be set up to form a temporary passageway for the young actors as they enter or leave the stage.

STIPPLING

One kind of painted scenery furnishes a simplified type of stage setting. This is known as stippled scenery and consists of flats or screens on which are painted a variegated color effect. The scenery committee may produce a new stage setting at small expense by this process. The canvas of a shabby interior for instance, which has been made whole by patching or replacement, should be given two coats of a neutral tone such as gray or gray blue—for example, Alabastine No. 54. If new muslin or canvas is used it should be primed before it is painted. The entire surface of the canvas should then be daubed over with small brush spots of several harmonious colors, for example, orange, green, and purple. These "dabs" may also be easily applied by the flat surface of a sponge which has been cut in half. Still another method is to use a large brush from which the paint is spattered on the canvas. For this purpose, Alabastine positive colors No. 10, No. 5, No. 98 will serve. Show card colors come in more brilliant hues and offer a wider range of choice. A light finishing coat of gray should finally be applied over all. This process, also called pointillage, creates a unique effect of an all-over color in a white light, and the appearance of varying colors under other lights, depending upon the light employed.

In a setting which employs simplified scenery, properties are used sparingly; but with careful discrimination. One or two objects only suggest the central idea,—a wall and fountain for a garden, an arch and window for a church.

Whether, then, the committee in charge constructs new scenery for the operetta, or whether it revamps the old scenery which it has at its disposal, the director should provide an appropriate and attractive scenic background for the action, the costumes, and the lighting effects of the operetta.

CHAPTER XIII

The Properties

Stage properties include the movable objects, stage decorations and furnishings, exclusive of the scenery, such as set trees, rocks, and furniture; also, articles which create an atmosphere or suggest some specific country, a period in history, or a time of year—such as flowers, lanterns, firearms, a spinning wheel, rugs, or various wall decorations, and in addition, the small paraphernalia which are to be used by the individual actors.

THE PROPERTY MAN

Since these items, commonly referred to as "props," are often numerous and are always important, it should be the work of one individual, the property man, to provide and care for them. A reliable student, who is not in the operetta, may be given this position. Whatever properties are used, whether they are made, borrowed, or purchased, they should be collected, looked after by the property man, and those which have been borrowed should be promptly returned after the performance.

THE PROPERTY LIST

The property man should go over the operetta carefully with the stage manager and compile a complete list of the properties which will be required, from the largest pieces of furniture to the smallest articles. Even though some of the principals may supply part of their own accessories, the property man should include these on his list and check them at the dress rehearsal as well as on the night of the final performance.

Failure to make a detailed list and to follow it often lead to embarrassing moments: The scene is a business office; a tense atmosphere has been created in the minds of the audience. At a critical moment the employer turns to send an important message. He reaches for the telephone—it is missing! Although the quick action of a player in the wings may bring the telephone to the desk and thus end the suspense, the spell has been broken and the illusion is gone.

Before the beginning of Act I the property man should assemble all the properties that are to be used during this act; these should be located on a table behind the scenes, at a place which will be convenient for the actors, but where they will be undisturbed by the chorus in their movements. The property man should remain at this point ready to hand to each character the required article. All off-stage business and all special effects other than the lighting should be looked after by the property man or by an assistant under his direction. At the end of Act I he will put away all the properties which have been used in this act, and carefully following his list he will place on the table all of the properties which are to be used in the next act, and so on.

ANACHRONISMS

An interior scene is often made or marred by a single piece of furniture. The wicker furniture that is appropriate for a sun parlor cannot by any stretch of the imagination be employed to create the picture of a drawing room. The period to which a piece of stage property belongs should also be considered. A grandfather's clock and a cane-seated chair, or a hooked rug, a what-not, and a spinning-wheel give an unmistakable colonial atmosphere; but an anachronism would result were a piano or a victrola introduced into the scene. The inclusion of a modern pen or frying-pan in a scene representing the time of Robin Hood, an army rifle used in a frontier setting, or nineteenth-century station-

ery substituted for parchment are other illustrations of this
point.

COLONIAL INTERIOR

ADAPTING PROPERTIES

Cretonne covers often permit the use of certain pieces of
furniture which would otherwise be inappropriate because
of style or color.   A coat of paint will make used furniture
suitable for use again.   A cheap table of the right design
if given a coat of lacquer will be more satisfactory than a
piece of solid mahogany; and will better withstand rough
and careless treatment, as for example when a glass of water
is accidently overturned.   Most pieces of furniture look
better under the artificial light than they do by daylight.
A common picture frame and a worn piece of statuary will
be greatly improved by a coat of bronze.   A very ordinary
painting when given a coat of dead-lac to which a tinge of

green or brown has been added, will take on the appearance of age. A painting or a mirror will relieve a large unattractive wall space. They should be hung on wires which are firmly attached to the frame of the flat scenery. In view of the fact that a mirror may reflect the footlights, the borders, or the audience, it should be hung with care. The *effect* of a mirror may be obtained by the use of an empty frame with a skillful arrangement of drapes at the side and at the back to give the appearance of reflection.

SCREENS AND DRAPES

Draperies before a window are always effective; these should be appropriate in color and texture; heavy draperies should be used for elaborate halls and dainty prints for a simple room. Screens are both decorative and useful, particularly on a small stage where entrances are limited: ordinary burlap or wooden screens may be easily and artistically decorated by the addition of gilt paper, or by the use of figured wall paper to represent tapestry.

SECURING PROPERTIES

In searching for ideas which will add realism to a stage setting, the property man should study reproductions in the art magazines. The *National Geographic* and magazines devoted to interior decoration such as the *House Beautiful*, together with books of travel, will also be serviceable along this line.

The property man will do well to present the required list of properties to the cast or chorus. Some of them will have suggestions as to where certain articles may be found. Negatively stated, familiar school property is least desirable for stage use. These pieces of furniture are so definitely associated in the minds of the audience with the familiar surrounding that they will contribute little toward the creation of an illusion. New furniture, a victrola, or a radio may sometimes be borrowed from local firms if credit for the courtesy is given on the program. Used furniture may be borrowed from friends of the cast or chorus, or rented from a second-hand dealer. Certain small articles which may be purchased at the ten-cent store will serve as well as expensive pieces. In a small prairie city the department store, at the suggestion of the school supervisor, has made a practice of setting aside from year to year the various window decorations: arches, lattice works, palms, and flowers, for the use of the local school in staging its operettas. In some of the larger cities it is possible to rent certain stage properties which cannot be borrowed or constructed. Firms which rent costumes frequently carry a supply of unusual stage furniture and properties. One individual should be made responsible for the care and return of all articles which have been borrowed. A word of caution to the stage hands and to the amateur actors may avoid permanent injury to property that friends have been generous enough to loan.

BUILDING PROPERTIES

The ingenuity and skill of the stage carpenter will be found equal to many demands if he is given a clear idea of just what is required and sufficient advance notice as to when it will be needed. A most creditable suit of armor with accompanying helmet, shield, and long spear, may be constructed with very little labor. On a costume-frame, easily obtainable from a clothing merchant, may be hung a coat and riding breeches which are then covered with silver paper. The shield may be made of pasteboard and the spear of beaver board. A few wire supports may be required at certain points. The stage carpenter who has a fertile mind will also be able to provide exterior scenes with new properties. In a wood scene, a rustic arbor made from saplings or of one-half-inch lumber and covered with artificial vines and flowers will add greatly to the stage picture and furnish

A PROPERTY SUGGESTION

(A prairie schooner made of beaver board—Excellent grouping)

a new entrance. A well curb, a forge, a set rock, and old-style lamp post, or a low hedge built of lath and twined with flowers and leaves, which is most effective if placed down-stage, suggest the countless properties available for the expenditure of but little time and effort. In a Japanese setting, a torii of lumber or compo-board and a two-wheeled rickshaw are most appropriate for an exterior scene; branches to which artificial cherry blossoms are tied make suitable decorations for interior and exterior scenes alike. A miniature pagoda up-stage, round tea baskets swung on either end of a long pole, a tea table on which are several bowls, and a fortune-teller's table form a distinctly Chinese picture. A tepee, canoe paddles, a set of horns, bows and arrows, fur rugs, and crude pottery create the atmosphere of an Indian scene. A shipboard scene with a deck rail, a Ford-tire life preserver, a capstan and a rope ladder, a funnel of compo-board, deck chairs, and perhaps a practical cabin needs only a marine backdrop to create an atmosphere redolent of the sea itself.

PRACTICAL PROPERTIES

Practical properties are those which may actually be used, handled, or moved. They make possible interesting stage business and are valuable additions to the stage equipment. A practical rock may be built with a solid box as the basis. The box should be not less than 36 inches on its shortest side and not more than 12 or 14 inches high. On three of its sides triangular pieces 9 x 9 should be nailed. Several small sacks filled tightly with paper should be laid on top of the box. Over these sacks chicken wire should be tacked and canvas or muslin stretched over all. The surface should then be painted gray or brown with splotches of color to simulate moss and lichens. A similar frame built with a curved surface, covered with sacking or burlap, and painted green, will make a grassy mound. The effect of a grass plot is produced by the use of a green carpet or a few grass mats. These latter, however, are somewhat expensive; a $3\frac{1}{2}$ x 7 carpet, for example, costs five dollars. In a Kansas

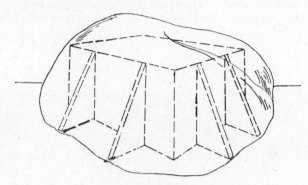

A PRACTICAL ROCK

school, the boys of the manual training department built a fence by nailing young saplings to 1 x 4's running lengthwise, with short diagonals to prevent collapse. This fence

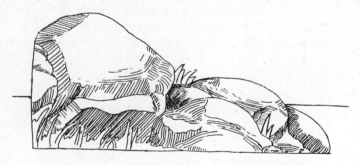

A ROCK "FLAT"

was made in three sections; two were placed end to end, and a rustic gate was hung between them and the remaining section. Additional action and stage pictures were thus

made possible.   A practical rope swing wound with paper
flowers and attached to the gridiron or stage ceiling gives
newness and movement to a woodland scene.   Practical
stumps may be easily constructed of nail kegs covered with

A PRACTICAL TOADSTOOL

burlap and then painted brown.   To make a practical toadstool, the base, the upright, and a top with scalloped edges
should be cut from wood and nailed together.   The top
should be covered first with excelsior and then with canvas.

PROPERTIES AT REHEARSALS

To facilitate the movements of the actors and to familiarize them with the location or use of the several properties
with which they will have to deal, the stage manager should,
at an early rehearsal, mark on the floor the location of the
larger objects, or better, indicate these by a chair, a box,
etc.   Small articles, which are to be used by an actor should
be in his hands at every rehearsal; a substitute article, such
as a stick for a sword, will serve the purpose until the required property is obtained.

The number and suitability of the stage properties of

various kinds will be dependent upon the combined knowledge and ingenuity of the stage manager and the property
man.   The properties will be just as novel, just as appropriate for the operetta that is being given, and just as
artistic as these two care to spend the time and effort in
making them.

CHAPTER XIV

Costumes

CLOTHES AND THE ACTOR

In the creation of the various stage pictures, the stage manager should realize that the costumes play a large part. Not only are they important to the audience in creating the desired stage illusion, and in providing for them a source of enjoyment, through color and design, but costumes also have a very real value in their influence upon the amateur actor himself. For, in some measure, stage dress aids the young actor in realizing and expressing his characterization of a part; for instance, royal garments make a girl a queen, and the sailor costume creates in the mind of the boy who wears it the spirit of a jolly tar.

COSTUMES AN INDEX

Costumes are the first feature of the stage picture to attract the eye. They should therefore, receive equal emphasis with other phases of the preparation. The clothes which the actors wear on the stage should tell very definitely the *kind* of characters they are. The hat alone differentiates the bandit from the baker. Before a line is spoken, the audience recognizes the prince and the pauper. As in everyday life we judge a man somewhat by his appearance, so, on the stage, we form our first impression of a player through his costume. Just as in the other steps of preparation, so in the matter of costuming, the stage manager should begin early to make plans. The first step will be the study of the story, the country, the historical period, and any other details which have a bearing upon the question of the costumes.

AN EASTERN PRINCE AND PRINCESS
(An example of perfect costuming)

ESSENTIALS IN COSTUMES

The stage manager, or the designer of a costume, should realize that he is not supposed to copy exactly in every detail the mode or fashion of the clothing of a certain period. Rather is he, through the use of characteristic design and trimmings and from suitable material, to produce a silhouette or outline consistent with the spirit of the period. An American gentleman of 1800 is readily recognized by his leather slippers, silk stockings, satin waistcoat, evening dress-coat, expanse of white shirt-front, stock, and white standing collar—all surmounted by a beaver hat. Such a costume would also be characteristic of a gentleman of England, Ireland, and France during the nineteenth century. By substituting tights for the knee breeches and making such slight changes as touches of lace at the neck and sleeves, jewels in the shoe buckles and waistcoat buttons, this costume, elegant in its every detail, would serve for a Beau Brummel. Again, by substituting white knee breeches, and a blue coat with epaulets and a tricorn hat we have a Napoleonic costume.

PERIOD COSTUMES

If the setting of the operetta is historical, the stage manager should make sure that the costumes are in the mode of the particular period designated in the operetta. Inaccuracy in this regard is easily avoided if reference is made to a nearby library, where illustrated books and magazines will furnish many suggestions for costumes of the different periods in history. Even the small-town library will include a good encyclopedia; in this the stage manager should look up such topics as Costumes, Armor, Middle Ages, Puritan, etc. The following volumes, if not obtainable locally, may be secured by mail from a nearby city library: an illustrated copy of *Ben Hur*, and Tissot's *Life of Christ*, both of which will suggest costumes for biblical scenes; MacGreggor's *Story of Rome* or Meyer's *General History* picture costumes of the ancient Rome and Gauls; Guizot's *France and England* gives the dress of the early Britains; and the illustrated editions of *Miles Standish*, Godey's *Lady Book* and *Hero Tales From American History*, by Theodore Roosevelt, illustrate costumes for the different periods of American history. *The Book of the American Spirit*, illustrated by Howard Pyle, will be found helpful in designing costumes of the colonial period. Frederic Remington's drawings of cow-boys and pioneers are authentic; the costume of the Indian in Longfellow's *The Song of Hiawatha*, illustrated by this artist, is unsurpassed for accuracy and detail.

PRESENT-DAY COSTUMES

The preparation for costuming an operetta, the scene of which is laid in the present day, would seem at first thought to be a simple matter. The fact, however, that the audience is so thoroughly familiar with the costumes of its own day necessitates extreme care on the part of the stage manager. The costumes should be faultless in color, fit, and design. Furthermore, he must see to it that the ensemble—the general effect created by the costumes of the chorus and the principals—is characterized by uniformity. In a chorus composed of girls dressed alike, their skirts should match or harmonize in color, and should be of an equal distance from the floor; their shoes should be similar in style and color, and their stockings should be of the same shade and quality.

NATIONAL AND OTHER COSTUMES

For an operetta, the scene of which is foreign, the stage manager will find many suggestions in the *National Geographic*, *Travel*, *Asia*, and the *Mentor*. These and similar magazines contain representative costumes of all countries. Almost every small library will include one or more volumes on costumes which will be of real service to any one who is planning to produce an operetta.   Howard Pyle's *Book of Pirates* and his *Merry Adventures of Robin Hood* are full of suggestions for colorful costumes of bold buccaneers and brigands.

DUTCH IN EVERY DETAIL

CHILDREN'S COSTUMES

Excellent ideas for costumes for primary operettas will be obtained from the volumes illustrated by Kate Greenaway and Jessie Wilcox Smith.   Illustrations by the latter will be found in Alcott's *Little Women* and *Old Fashioned Girl;* Chapin's *Now-A-Day Fairy Book,* and Moore's *'Twas The Night Before Christmas.*   Clever suggestions will also be found in Rose O'Neil's *Kewpie Primer* and Peter Newell's *Pictures and Rhymes.*   Still another illustrator of children's subjects is Arthur Rackam, whose excellent pictures afford many interesting suggestions in Barrie's *Peter Pan*, Evan's *Cinderella*, Grimm's *Hänsel and Gretel*, Lamb's *Tales From Shakespeare*, La Motte's *Undine*, and Swift's *Gulliver's Travels*. Ideas for fanciful and animal costumes are numerous in *Peter Rabbit* and others of the Uncle Remus stories which are so charmingly illustrated by A. B. Frost. The Dennison Crepe Paper Company, Chicago and Boston, publishes books with pictures of costumes for fairies, flowers, and Mother Goose characters. These books contain minute instructions for making the costumes and should be examined before costumes are rented or materials for delicate effects are chosen.

EXPENDITURES FOR COSTUMES

As in similar undertakings, a budget plan will be found advisable in staging an operetta. Before any money is allotted for the rental of costumes or for material from which to make them, the stage manager, in consultation with the business manager, should estimate the approximate cost of the scenery, costumes, advertising, properties, lighting, etc. Inadequate amounts spent on any of these items may detract seriously from the effectiveness of the final performance; whereas extravagant expenditures are quite likely to result in a deficit.

APPORTIONING EXPENSES

Having determined the approximate amount to be expended for costumes, this sum should be divided in such a way that a few characters or a single group will not outshine in costume the rest of the cast and chorus. How disappointing it is to the audience—and perhaps to the children themselves—to have a grade operetta in which the principals, the fairies, and the other child players are exquisitely costumed, suddenly spoiled by the appearance of a chorus of children who are supposed to represent dainty, lovely flowers, but who, on account of their bedraggled hit-and-miss costumes actually look like faded, droopy, much-be-wilted posies! Such unevenness of costuming is often the consequence of a too liberal expenditure of funds for the important characters; sometimes it is the result of a division of labor without proper supervision; again it happens because of eleventh-hour haste. Whatever the cause may be, it should not occur.

RENTING COSTUMES

Where expense is not a first consideration, costumes for the cast and chorus may be rented from a professional costumer. If the operetta is not well known and is not a standardized production, such as Planquette's *Chimes of Normandy* or Gilbert and Sullivan's *Pinafore*, the stage manager, in ordering the costumes, should give the full details as to the setting of the operetta, the requirements for the principals, the character and number of the chorus costumes.

The least expensive procedure is to rent the costumes of the principals and make those of the chorus—providing a company can be found which will give a satisfactory price on this basis. Occasionally a better price can be obtained if in addition to the costumes for the principals, all or part of the chorus costumes are rented. The rental of costumes ranges from $1.00 to $3.00 apiece for a single performance, a reduction being made in case of a second night's use. The express is paid by the renter. If the costume firm is notified in advance, it will send costumes in ample time for the dress rehearsal. Almost all costumers can supply oriental, gypsy, fairy, colonial, Indian, or animal costumes. The objection which many people have to using rented costumes is more fancied than real; for dry-cleaning and the proper care of costumes is a part of the regular business procedure of reputable firms.

A costume plate or sketch will be valuable in securing the exact costumes which are required. Such a sketch should be merely an outline of the figure on which the outstanding features of the costumes are suggested and the colors indicated by paints.

MAKING COSTUMES

Many chorus costumes are so simple as to material and design that they may be made at home. Take, for example,

GYPSY
(Costume made from old bandanna handkerchiefs. Kindergarten beads)

an operetta in which the chorus girls may be dressed in simple peasant garb—short full skirts, laced bodices, and white blouses. The materials for these costumes are inexpensive and may easily be fashioned into attractive and appropriate costumes by the mothers of the children or by the domestic science department. One particular advantage of making such simple costumes is that it is possible to carry out a uniformity of color scheme—a uniformity, which is sometimes unobtainable in rented costumes. If, however, the cost of materials for elaborate or difficult costumes amounts to more than the rental of these costumes it would be far better to rent them.

Fortunate indeed is the director who has the assistance of a capable home economics teacher in designing and taking charge of the actual making of costumes. Together, these two, after having decided upon the amount of money to be spent for costumes, may select the materials. Under the supervision of the instructor, all the costumes should be cut out, ready to be finished by members of sewing classes, or in the school operetta to be sent home for the children's mothers to make. If the mothers are to finish the costumes, sketches or pictures showing exactly how the finished costumes should look will be of great assistance to them. In the smaller towns, even the principals' costumes are often made at home. The author recalls an example of economical and effective costuming of a high-school production of *The Mikado*, the final rehearsals of which he was called in to coach. The director in question had handed over to the instructor in sewing and costume design the whole problem of costuming the cast and chorus. Under her guidance, the pupils in the various classes had made Japanese kimonos and coats of simple materials. On these kimonos, they had blocked in, or stencilled, gorgeous and beautiful designs in an infinite variety of coloring. The resulting stage picture was far more beautiful than rented costumes would have produced.

Costumes which are made by persons outside of the school should be finished and brought for approval to the director or the stage manager at least one week before the production. If the work is not completed until the night of the dress rehearsal, the rehearsal is certain to be delayed.

"THREE LITTLE MAIDS" FROM *THE MIKADO*
(An amateur production)

Furthermore the cast and the director will probably become nervous as a result of refitting costumes that could have been made satisfactory had the garments been finished and inspected a week before. So, whether the costumes are rented, whether they are made at home or at school, they should be properly inspected and approved in ample time for the dress rehearsal.

COMMERCIAL PATTERNS

For additional information relative to selecting and making costumes, the stage manager should consult the pattern books of commercial pattern companies, such as the *Pictorial Review*, *McCall's*, and the *Ladies' Home Journal*. These companies furnish accurate patterns for historic, national, and fantastic costumes. Nor should the stage manager overlook the Copley prints, the Perry pictures, and various other reproductions of art subjects.

TAKING MEASURES

Whether costumes are to be ordered from a professional costumer or are to be made, all measurements should be carefully taken. Sleeve lengths, length of trousers, waist measurements, width of shoulders, bust and hip measurements are essential. The length of skirts should be determined from the floor as well as from the waistline.

COLOR OF MATERIALS

If costumes are to be made, the individual who chooses the materials should take into consideration the weight and texture of the fabric,—but even more particularly the color. Selections should not be made in a shop where the white lights give to fabrics a far different shade from that given by stage illumination. He should take several bolts on approval and make his final choice only after he has seen the material at night under the lighting which is to be used at the performance. In ordering or having costumes made, the stage manager should take into account not only the harmony of color which must exist between two important characters, but also the general effect of the scene as a whole. What would otherwise be a perfect stage picture may be ruined by a glaring bodice which clashes with all of the other costumes on the stage.

SUBSTITUTE MATERIALS

Under stage lights, many inexpensive fabrics serve as excellent substitutes for costly materials. In the selection of such materials the stage manager should take into account not only the color and the manner in which the material will drape, but also the texture or character of the weave. Sateen, tarlatan, and figured cretonnes may be substituted for the more expensive satins, chiffons, and brocaded silks. In using the cheaper materials, such as tarlatan or cheese-cloth, it should not be forgotten that the addition of gathers, tucks, lace, and other trimmings will divert attention from the quality of the material and will give the illusion of more expensive fabrics. Under nimble fingers, King Cole's velvet and ermine may be reproduced by the use of canton flannel and white cotton on which black spots are painted. The queen's heavy satin need be nothing more than a lustrous sateen, and her maids may be daintily gowned in flowered silkoline.

DYEING

Again, in considering the use of inexpensive materials as substitutes, the stage manager should investigate the possibilities of the use of dyes—provided he may be certain of an assistant who can and will take the responsibility for this work. However, it should be said at this point that the process may be more expensive for novices in the end than would be the purchasing of colorful silkolines, chintzes, etc.

In buying muslin which is to be dyed, care should be taken that the dressing in the material will **not** prevent the absorption of the dye.   Cotton crepe, cheese-cloth, voile, and sateen may be dipped; but muslin is most effectively dyed by appling the color with a brush.   A safe procedure is to experiment with a sample of the material which is to be dyed before purchasing a quantity.

Ordinary dyeing of material gives a flat uninteresting effect, an effect which can be overcome by a process known as top-dyeing.   For example, a material is first dyed blue, and then topped with red; this treatment gives a vivid color not obtainable by the use of a single purple dye.   Again, a material dyed yellow and top-dyed with red will have a life and depth of color not secured by a single treatment.   If the material to be dyed is twisted so that the red dye will have a different density, an excellent red gold will be the result.   Cotton materials dipped in a brilliant dye and then top-dyed unevenly with a dark purple, red, or green, take on something of the depth and richness of velvet.   Unusual effects are obtained by tying portions of the material in knots and then dipping them into the dye—the result being a pattern of irregular shadings.   In dyeing material it is in most instances better to dye the complete garment than the material in the bulk.   Unique effects are obtainable by painting designs on the dyed garment.   Garments which have been dyed should be hung on wire hangers; wood fixtures absorb dye.   It should be added that dyes obtained from small drug stores are not always satisfactory.   The reader is referred to Agnes Brooks Young's *Stage Costuming*, published by MacMillian, which gives specific directions for different methods of dyeing.   Another excellent reference book is *Costuming A Play* by Grimbell-Wells, published by The Century Company.   With all standard commercial dyes come directions which may safely be followed.

OWNERSHIP

When the parents have paid for them, the costumes,

of course, belong to the children; however, since for the children they have value only in connection with a stage production, some schools reimburse the parents for the cost of the materials and retain the costumes. Under these circumstances, as well as when the school has paid for them out of the proceeds, the costumes belong to the school and should be carefully put away for future use. The director or supervisor who inaugurates the plan of having a room in which the costumes of various school entertainments may be stored, will, in a few seasons, not only save for the school an amount of money equal to the proceeds of a successful operetta, but he will eliminate for himself much concern in connection with providing costumes for future dramatic productions.

CARE OF COSTUMES

The effectiveness of the costumes at the final performance will be greatly increased if the amateur is given several important instructions along this line: first, every part of the costume must be put on and removed carefully; second, the different parts of the costumes should be folded neatly or hung on hangers; third, all accessories should be kept with the costume to which they belong; fourth, extreme care should be exercised that no rough treatment seriously damage or mar the appearance of the costume for which the individual is responsible. Unnecessary vigorous exercise off-stage may prove embarrassing for some one in a tight-fitting garment, and may cause an awkward delay in the performance. A lively one-time Bob Acres in *The Rivals* tore his riding breeches just a moment before his entrance cue; a safety-pin, hastily employed, served its purpose. Following his exit, however, Bob nonchalantly sat down on a mahogany table; a fellow actor pulled him off, and in an instant the pin had done twenty dollars worth of damage to the table, a valuable piece of furniture which had been loaned for the occasion by a friend of the stage manager.

Costumes do not appear the same under stage lighting as they do in daylight or the ordinary electric lights of the home. The designer of stage costumes will add much to the final stage picture if he understands or learns the effect of artificial light on colors of costumes. For example, all colors except red are changed by red light. Amber, often substituted for white, gives a grey cast to blues or greens. It is important to remember that dark colors show up best against a light background, and light colors against a dark background. The latter suggests distance, whereas the former gives the appearance of decreased size. The surest method for determining the best color effects in costumes is to try out as has been suggested the different colors on the stage under the lights which are to be used.

Important parts of every costume, although they are not garments, are the accessories and accoutrements, such as head-dresses, shoes, jewelry, fans, wands, etc. These should be taken into account by the persons designing the costume, for they also help to make the illusion more real, and to enhance the personalities of the characters portrayed. Care in having accessories match the costume will avoid such incongruities as a Japanese maid shuffling across the stage in high-heeled pumps, or a Puritan matron moving demurely about in a fancy, lace-trimmed apron.

Head-dresses of various types and styles can be created by taking buckram, or similar material used by milliners, and filling it with sizing (Cf. Chapter XII). After the material has been steamed until it is pliable, it can be shaped over a mold and then stiffened by the addition of more size.

It is usually found desirable to use two or even three
thicknesses of buckram, from which, as a basis, a crown, a
helmet, or a Dutch cap can be constructed. Visors and
plumes cut out of the same material will hold their shape
when wired, and furnish the requisite trimming for the
helmets. The helmets should be bronzed or polished with
graphite. A coating of shellac inside will protect them
from perspiration. If there are no large buckles available
for the colonial gentleman's slippers, they may be made
from pasteboard, given a coat of silver paint, and fastened
by means of an elastic band over an ordinary pair of oxfords.
A few strokes of the paint brush will convert old shoes into
beautiful Greek or Roman sandals, or a pair of stocking
feet, dyed to match the costume and pulled over a pair of
gymnasium shoes will serve. Deft touches can transform
hats into helmets, beaver-board into swords, black oilcloth
into pirate boot-tops; art oilcloth is effective in leather
jerkins, in tops for cavalier boots, etc.

A burlap coat of armor may be given a realistic touch
by painting it with powdered graphite which has been
mixed with glue to give it consistency; when dry the surface
should be polished or brushed with a rag which has been
dipped in dry graphite. A very small amount of silver
powder gently blown over the surface before the glue has
dried will give an effect of spots highly polished. The stage
manager should, of course, warn his actors of the unsub-
stantial character of such specially designed bits of costume,
and of the consequent necessity of care in handling them.

WEARING OF COSTUMES

Not only should the amteur actor be instructed as to the
proper care of his costume—he should also be shown the
importance of wearing it correctly. That is to say, the
Quaker miss and the court lady of Queen Elizabeth's time
will wear their costumes in a manner befitting their parts—

a manner which will be manifested not only in their poise and posture, but in their walk as well.

While costumes do not make the actor nor the operetta, we see that they do play an important part in creating for the audience, as well as for the performers, the illusive but necessary atmosphere of stage realism.

Too much attention and preparation, then, cannot be given to the individual and collective costuming of the cast and chorus; for "As a man thinketh in his heart, so is he";— as a character is costumed, so, too, to a certain extent at least, will his acting be.

CHAPTER XV

The Make-Up

Although practical experience is essential to enable one to produce results of a professional kind, a knowledge of certain fundamentals of making up will enable the inexperienced but observant director to carry out creditably this part of his work. His first step in preparation should be to study the facial characteristics of individuals of different ages and nationalities, noting the variations in lines and features which result from age and from the play of varying emotions. If the beginner be wise he will go *very slowly* in the application of make-up, for, whether on the stage or on the street, "they are as sick that surfeit with too much, as they that starve with nothing."

EXPERT ASSISTANCE

As in other phases of preparation for the operetta, so in that of make-up, foresight is necessary; all arrangements should be made well in advance of the performance. If the school is located in or near a large city, the easiest method is to secure the services of a professional make-up man who will bring with him everything necessary except cold cream and soft rags or towels. Any firm which rents costumes will be able to provide the services of such a professional. Again, competent assistance may often be obtained from the dramatic department of a nearby college. However secured, such assistance will not only lift a load of responsibility from the director's shoulders but it will assure a far more satisfactory appearance of the cast and chorus.

A MAKE-UP OUTFIT

If the services of a professional make-up artist cannot be obtained, the first thing for the director to do is to go over this matter of make-up with a local druggist at least two weeks before the performance. Theatrical make-up is carried by nearly all drug-stores, and any required materials which they do not have in stock can be ordered. The grease paints used for foundation come in more than twenty numbered colors. The director should go over these carefully, taking into consideration the number of people to be made up, so that he may order the right amount. Whereas cold cream will be needed in a large quantity, only a limited amount of grease paint should be ordered, for one stick of it will go a long way. A fairly complete make-up outfit will include the following items: theatrical cold-cream; foundation grease paints, in several different shades; liners —black, brown, white, blue, and red; theatrical powder in colors to correspond to the foundation paints; eyebrow pencils, in brown, black, and blue; theatrical lipstick, in light and dark carmine; theatrical wet and dry rouge; spirit gum; alcohol; make-up putty; crepe hair of several shades; powder puffs; and toothpicks with which to apply lines.

EXPERIMENTATION

Several times before the dress rehearsal the person who has been put in charge of make-up should experiment on the important principals under the lighting effects to be employed. No two people require the same treatment. What may appear satisfactory for one face will be found insufficient and expressionless for another. Members of the chorus may be made up by assistants for whom a sample make-up has been done by someone having more experience. Two assistants should be sufficient; the result will be far more satisfactory and uniform than if several people try to help.

Straight make-up is employed when the actor plays the part of a character of his own age, sphere, and nationality; in grade school operettas, the children are so young that their tiny features need only a slight intensifying of the "red and white, nature's own sweet and cunning hand laid on."

Straight make-up is relatively simple. First the cold cream should be rubbed in evenly and sparingly; any excess which the skin fails to absorb should be wiped off gently so as to leave the feeling but not the appearance of grease. Then a *small* amount of rouge should be put on the cheek bones and spread carefully until it blends into the natural flesh tint. A light touch gives the smoothest result. Failure to blend the rouge out toward the eyes and jaw leaves a sharp line at the edges of the red daub which gives a hideous effect—an effect which is in no way preferable to the face devoid of make-up—deathly white under the strong rays of the stage light. A touch of rouge should be placed at the center of the chin. With a crimson lip-stick, the cupid's bow of the upper lip can be emphasized, and the lower lip outlined with the same shade, *care being taken not to spread the mouth too wide*. A touch of the eyebrow pencil, a light line of black on the edges of the upper and lower lids, then for brilliance a tiny speck of bright carmine lip-stick placed with the point of a toothpick in each corner of the eyes, a very delicate dusting over all of flesh powder, and the make-up is completed. This straight make-up is all that is necessary for girls of any age, and for boys up to the high school age. The above is known as a dry make-up. Chorus members usually need only this type of make-up. Frequently the faces of high-school boys take the make-up better if a grease paint foundation is applied after the cold cream, and before the rouge, lip-stick, and eyebrow pencil are used. The finger tips should be used in applying grease paint, which should be rubbed in well. The tone to be used (such as healthy sunburn, ruddy, and olive) will be determined by the character to be portrayed. The catalogue will help one to decide the proper tone. If one shade fails to produce the desired result, another may be blended with it.

CHARACTER MAKE-UP

Before he begins making-up for character parts, the make-up artist will find it profitable to study pictures and to observe people about him. He should then determine upon and keep definitely in mind the character he wishes to portray. Successful character make-up requires painstaking care and practical experience. For example: an old man is apt to squint his eyes until they are mere slits; his forehead wrinkles; his cheeks sink in; his chin sags; his mouth assumes a downward droop or his lips are held askew.

These and similar features should be accentuated by make-up. Over the cold-cream foundation should be spread grease paint of the correct shade for old age, well rubbed in with the finger tips. With gray, blue, or brown lining-pencils should be drawn in the horizontal wrinkles across the forehead, the sagging lines where they naturally appear —from the nostril to the corner of the mouth and on either side of the chin to the lower jaw—and the crow's-feet at the corners of the eyes. Hollows may be accented with gray and carried down into the neck, if the costume is open at the throat. The ears require the same make-up that the face receives. Hands are often overlooked by the amateur, with resultant loss in character portrayal. Hands for old people are made up as follows: after grease paint of the same shade as that used on the face has been applied, the veins of the hands are outlined with blue or gray liners, and the knuckles and the inside of the fingers are darkened.

Teeth are blocked out with a black wax made for the purpose. If none is available, the tooth must be dried, then covered with black eyebrow pencil. The wax, however, is preferable. Warts and freak features are made from a special wax—"nose putty." This wax is applied in the same manner in which crepe hair is stuck on. It should be toned in with the foundation grease paint. The spot where the wax is to be applied must be cleansed from grease paint by means of alcohol, and thoroughly dried. Make-up should be removed by applying several coats of theatrical cold-cream,—rubbing off each with a soft cloth. Never use soap and water.

EYEBROWS AND BEARDS

Crepe hair, which is used for eyebrows, mustaches, etc., comes in several different shades. Care should be exercised in matching the natural hair of the character to be portrayed. If the required shade cannot be obtained, a lighter rather than a darker shade should be employed. Spirit gum, used to stick crepe hair to the skin, will not hold if applied over grease paint. The spot on the face where the false hair is to be fastened should, therefore, be cleansed by rubbing it with a piece of cotton soaked in alcohol, allowed to dry, and then painted with spirit gum. When this gum is almost dry, the hair may be stuck on. Alcohol is used to dissolve the gum when the make-up is removed. In making up with a full beard, begin with the burnsides. Work the crepe hair straight and thin with the fingers, using pieces of hair longer than necessary, and then stick them well into the natural hair, so that there is no line between the natural hair and the crepe hair. Leave a space between the ear and the crepe hair. A thin piece of the false hair is next gummed underneath the chin, the hair coming forward; this piece should never be omitted. Next attach a piece of the crepe hair on the chin, letting it extend downward from the lower lip. After all of these pieces are attached, they should be trimmed carefully so that they will be in keeping with the character.   A mustache, regardless of how small it is, should always be put on in two pieces. This allows the small triangle of flesh on the upper lip and makes speaking much easier.   The natural eyebrow, if very heavy, can be rubbed with white grease paint and combed the wrong way, or the foundation paint over the eye brow may be removed with alcohol and crepe hair attached. Crepe hair, before it is applied to the face, should first be pulled and worked very thin with the fingers.

BLACK FACE

If the cast calls for a black-face part and the application of commercial burnt-cork paste is obnoxious to the person playing the part, an effective make-up is obtained by patting in theatrical black powder upon the cold cream which has been first rubbed in.   Again the leg of a black silk stocking makes a satisfactory substitute.   The upper part of the stocking should be gathered into as small a circle as possible and sewed together firmly.   It is then pulled down well over the head and allowed to cover the face and come down well over the neck.   Slits for the eyes should be cut and then overcast well to keep the cut edges from fraying. Another slit cut for the mouth may be bound in red satin ribbon, so as to give the effect of full red lips.

Elves and goblins, fascinating little fellows, in snug-fitting union suits dyed green, black or red, may be easily made up with stocking faces.   Flesh or nude shade stockings are best for this use.   After the stocking is drawn over the head, and the slits for eyes, mouth, and nose are cut and overcast, the fabric is firmly fastened around the neck. A few water color paints will help to bring the goblin to life.   Crepe hair or yarn may easily be sewed on the top and at the back for a wig effect, or a wicked-looking little cap can be pulled on to cover the back and top of the head. Colored mittens or gloves may be used for the hands.

WIGS

Wigs are very essential to character make-up. They may be rented from a costumer for a small sum—from fifty cents to two dollars each for a performance. In ordering wigs for men, the hat size should be given. For a woman's wig the head should be measured by allowing the tape to pass across the forehead and diagonally down and around the back of the head. Since costumers are not always prompt, disappointments may be avoided if the stage manager places the order for wigs several weeks before they will be required. Beards and wigs may be easily fumigated by putting them in the sunlight after sprinkling with formaldehyde.

Home-made wigs are not to be despised. A tight-fitting cap on the order of a Freshman cap can be used as a foundation for a home-made wig; to this, yarn, crepe hair, or even hempen rope which has been unravelled can be securely sewed. A colonial gentleman may wear a wig which has been made on the same sort of foundation, and which is covered with bleached lamb's wool trimmed to the desired shape and tied into a queue with black silk. Lamb's wool may be obtained at a drug store, a four ounce package for thirty-five cents. Cotton batting will serve as a substitute, though it is less satisfactory. When the wig fails to cover the natural hair, grease paint and powder should be used to block out all that shows on the forehead, the neck, or behind the ears.

Cornstarch or talcum powder dusted into the hair gives an effect of a white wig. All wigs, particularly home-made ones, present the best appearance if they are worn with a head-dress of some kind.

THE MAKE-UP ROOM

The room in which make-up is applied should be provided with two or three tables of ample size which are covered with clean paper. The room should be provided with several chairs and some good mirrors hung where the light strikes directly, one of them being a full length mirror, if possible. There should, of course, be running water in the room.

Much could be added to this brief discussion of make-up, but enough has been said to show that a crude application of make-up can do much toward detracting from the artistic appearance of even the best acted operetta. Obviously, then, a really artistic use of make-up should serve to put the finishing *touch* on a first-class performance.

CHAPTER XVI

The Lighting

If one will recall the dramatic productions which stand out in his experience he will remember certain scenes in which the most vital factor was a subtle change in the intensity of the light or a flood of color which enveloped the stage, the actors, and seemingly the audience itself. Contrary to common opinion, effects of this sort need not be confined to the theater of the large city; for, ethereal and evanescent as are these effects, they are merely the result of a properly manipulated lighting equipment which is already available or may be duplicated on the average stage of the small city.

INFLUENCE OF COLOR

Since the aim of the operetta is to create an illusion, the wise producer should study the effect of light and shadow and of colors and their combination. The importance of the psychological effect of color and the varying degrees of light are likely to be overlooked by the tonally-minded director. A cold blue light or a reddish glow have very definite effects upon the man of the street or the child at play. How much greater then is the influence of color upon the beholder who is already under the spell of the make-believe atmosphere of the stage.

COLOR EFFECTS

As is well known we see the form of an object as a result of the light rays which they reflect to the eye. The impression created by the rays reflected from a colored object, however, is quite variable, being dependent also upon the light rays which a given color absorbs. A blue light which falls upon an object does not of necessity cause this object to appear blue. A red coat under a red light appears red, but a yellow dress under a red light also appears red, whereas a green dress under a red light becomes black. A yellow dress in order to appear yellow must have a yellow light thrown upon it. The color effect of the costumes in an operetta is so kaleidoscopic that no single color will effectively illuminate a scene; it demands not only a skillful choice of color but also a discriminating blending of colored lights. When colors from electric lamps are blended, inter-mediate shades result, shades sometimes quite different from those obtained by the mixing of pigments. After having made the lighting equipment as adequate as circumstances will permit, the stage manager and electrician should learn by experimentation the most effective use of it.

STANDARD EQUIPMENT

Whereas it is customary to regard the lighting equipment of the local stage as a fixed quantity, the stage manager will discover that it may be materially altered and improved at a minimum effort and expense if he will but enlist the assistance of qualified persons. The simplest equipment for small auditoriums consists of the following lights.

FOOTLIGHTS

The footlights should be of a disappearing type, set in a metal trough that is painted white; the bulbs should be located six to eight inches apart and wired in three circuits. Footlights should extend only to a point within two or three feet of the proscenium arch—never entirely across the stage. They direct a strong light from below and intensify the facial expression of the persons on the stage. Since, however, no light in nature comes from such a source, the effect of footlights when improperly employed is to cause unnatural shadows on the floor or on the scenery. These shadows are so marked that the magnified movement and pantomime of a chorus as they show up against the backdrop may totally divert the attention of the audience. To counteract these shadows the stage manager should utilize border lights and floods.

The stage manager will discover that the total amount of light may be reduced through the use of fewer lamps in the footlights or of bulbs with smaller wattage; the smaller amount of light is preferably obtained, however, by a dimming device. Some of the most artistic productions of recent years have been done without the use of any footlights whatever. Since white light in the foots, or borders, gives an unnatural glare, amber colored bulbs are usually employed instead. The standard three-color equipment for footlights is amber, red, and blue. In a musical production, white footlights are most annoying, and often prevent a singer from seeing the baton of the director. An eleventh hour remedy will be provided by unscrewing temporarily the light which is found to be the chief cause of the interference.

BORDER LIGHTS

Border lights give a general illumination from above,—the natural source of light. The bulbs should be set nine inches from center to center in a metal trough which has been painted white for reflection. The number of sets of border lights to be used will depend upon the depth of the stage; a stage, twenty-five feet in depth, should have at least two borders. Border lights should extend the entire width of the stage and preferably three or four feet beyond the proscenium; if possible they should be so hung that they may be raised or lowered in order to balance the illumination from the footlights.

FLOOD LIGHTS

A flood or bunch light is a simple and effective means of lighting a given area with intensity and color. Adjustable flood lights, or "Olivetts," as they are called, cost about twenty dollars and are a valuable part of the lighting equipment for any stage. A flood light consists of a group of bulbs in a box, from which a lead wire plugs into a convenient floor pocket. Changes of color are secured through the use of removable screens which hold gelatin sheets.

MAKING A "FLOOD"

An ingenious stage carpenter can build a flood light at a small cost. This work and that of constructing any other electrical equipment should be supervised by an electrician and built in keeping with the insurance regulations. The carpenter should construct an open box 22 x 24, painting the inside with a white reflecting paint. On the two longer sides should be fastened strips underlaid with asbestos, to which the light sockets should be attached. The box should be provided with a recess or grooves in which to place the color frames. Unless it is made adjustable, this flood light should be mounted for convenience on a standard about five feet in height. It should however be detachable from the standard; when a flood of colored light is desired from a point above the stage, such as a moonlight scene, the box may be detached from the standard and suspended by lines from the gridiron. The frame which holds the gelatin sheets should be covered with a coarse wire screen to prevent the gelatin from cracking and curling when heated. Color frames with slide holders for gelatin sheets are purchaseable at sixty cents. Gelatin sheets require careful handling for they are affected by extreme heat, cold, or moisture. Fortunately they are inexpensive, costing twenty cents a sheet; they may be obtained in 19 x 21 and 20 x 24 sheets

from any house specializing in theatrical equipment.   As a
substitute for gelatin sheets, sheer colored fabrics or paper
screens may be used.   These, however, give only temporary

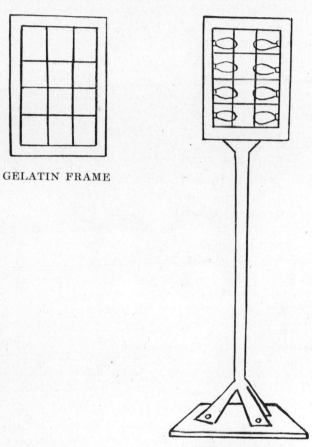

GELATIN FRAME

FLOOD LIGHT

service, and should be fireproofed, by using an alum solution.   Since they are far less translucent than gelatin,
stronger lamps should be employed.

STRIP LIGHTS

Strip lights are short portable rows of lights, similar to border lights, but varying in length from one to five feet. They lie flat and when they are masked by a hedge or a wall they may be used at any desired spot on the stage to give light from below. Strips are very effective for dawn and sunset scenes, and for lighting the faces of a group around a camp fire. They are purchaseable at a minimum cost, or they may be constructed by screwing light sockets on to a board to which has first been nailed a tin underlaid with asbestos.

SPOT LIGHT

A spot light is employed to focus an intense beam of light on an individual or on groups, in order to direct the atten-

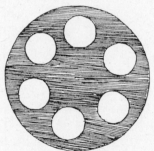

COLOR WHEEL

tion of the audience on them. These lights are installed in the balcony, in the wings, or in the motion picture booth. They may be moved at will in order to follow a performer or a small group about the stage. "Spots," as they are called, are equipped with color wheels—flat discs in which are made circular openings that are four to six inches in diameter. Each opening contains a gelatin of a different shade. These wheels cost five dollars, but they may be constructed quite cheaply by the aid of a tinsmith. A small spot light known as a "baby spot" may be purchased for fourteen dollars and will serve adequately for a small stage. A novel lighting effect may be secured through the use of a lantern slide in which the outline of a flower or heart has been cut. This lantern slide should be used in an ordinary stereoptican with a long focus lens. By the use of such a slide a dancer or a small group can be effectively silhouetted, as it were, in a frame against a light background. The size and shape of the spot is governed by a piece of opaque paper or cardboard which has been set in the slide carrier. Varied color effects may be obtained by placing mounted pieces of gelatin between the glasses of the lantern slide. If a diaphragm with irregular edges is interposed and the lens thrown slightly out of focus, what is known as a "Rembrandt effect" will be obtained instead of a well-defined spot. A strong flash-light, or the spot light of an automobile connected with a battery, may be made to serve if a commercial spot light is not obtainable.

DIMMERS

A dimming device by means of which varying degrees of light may be secured is a valuable feature in the lighting system of even a small stage. A dimmer may be used not only for increasing and diminishing light effects, but also for obtaining the exact amount of light desired in a scene which requires less than full light. Commerical dimmers adapted for small stages and controlling thirty 40-watt lamps, or forty-five 25-watt lamps, costs twelve dollars and fifty cents.

MAKING A DIMMER

However, a home-made dimmer may be constructed at a comparatively small cost. In making a dimmer, consideration should first be given to the resistance, voltage, and candle power of the light to be employed. Ordinarily a resistance equal to four times the resistance of the lamp load must be placed in series with the foots or borders, or with both, in order to dim completely either or both of these cir-

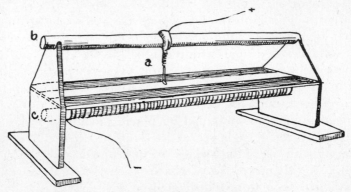

A DIMMING DEVICE

cuits.   The bulletin, L. D. 146 A, of the General Electric Company, on stage lighting, suggests: "Slide wire dimmers for temporary use may be simply constructed by winding a suitable length of resistance wire of the correct size on a piece of asbestos board or on an iron pipe (c) covered with a layer of sheet asbestos.   The slide is then properly mounted and covered except for the contact strip with a good dielectric cement and equipped with a rod (b) on which moves a slide contact (a)."   Full information regarding the properties of various resistance wire is obtainable from manufacturers.   An alert science department will be glad to cooperate in the making of such a dimming device.

A SIMPLE DEVICE

With the aid of a practical electrician a simple dimmer may be easily constructed from a small water-tight barrel and two short lengths of lead or galvanized iron pipe.   The cask is filled with a solution of water and common table salt; the amount of salt in the water determines the conductivity of the solution. In each of the opposite sides of the barrel's lid cut a hole to admit the piece of pipe. Insert pipe, *a*, through the hole at a slant so that it touches the bottom on the opposite side of the barrel. This pipe will be the

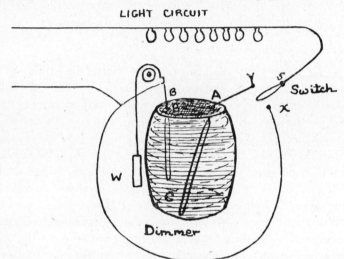

stationary electrode. The other pipe, *b*, from which runs a cord through an over-head pulley to a counterweight *w*, hangs in the second hole and serves as the movable electrode. The device is connected with the light circuit by means of a single pole, double-throw switch *s*. When the dimmer is not in use, the circuit is closed at *x*. When the switch is thrown to *y* and the pipe *b* is lowered so that it is in contact with *a*, the lights are of normal intensity. As *b* is separated from *a* the lights are gradually dimmed as the space at *c* is increased.

COLORING BULBS

In order to secure color effects, light bulbs may be dipped in coloring fluid known as Colorine or Transcolor, which is obtainable in ten colors. These coloring materials cost about one dollar and twenty-five cents for a half-pint, which amount is sufficient to color 125 bulbs. Lamps should be dipped while hot. This coating may be removed by dipping the bulbs in denatured alcohol or in a solution of colorine remover, which costs thirty-five cents per pound. Bulbs may also be colored by spraying them with lacquer.

LIGHTING SUGGESTIONS

The lighting employed in a scene should be sufficient to render the details of the scene apparent to the audience. At times, as in early dawn or twilight, only as much light should be employed as is necessary to suggest the outlines of the scene. In a night scene, only such details are illuminated as would be revealed by a candle or any other source of light which properly belongs in the setting. Phosphorescent paint is often used to give a glow to certain properties or costumes on a darkened stage. As has been said, the cyclorama in particular gives a remarkable illusion of distance and when proper lighting is combined with such a scenic background many charming and unusual effects can be obtained. Since stages, stage settings, lighting equipments, etc., vary greatly, it cannot be said that satisfactory lighting effects can be brought about by any fixed rules of procedure. Rather are they the result of study, preparation, and experimentation, the most important of which is experimentation—in other words, the trial and error methods.

UNIQUE EFFECTS

The ingenious electrician will utilize electricity for various effects. For instance, if a scene requires a forge, with flames coming out of it, any handy stage carpenter can construct it by taking a box of the required size, setting a small electric fan in the bottom of it, and supporting on a frame a cluster of red bulbs above the fan. Above the bulbs, and tied to

FRONT VIEW . FORGE END VIEW

the framework, should be fastened strips of red and yellow silk.   A realistic red flame will be simulated when the cluster

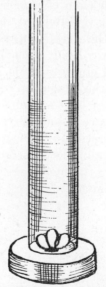

MARBLE COLUMN

of lights is turned on and the fan is set in motion.   If the effect of marble columns is desired, it can be produced by constructing a frame for the column, covering it with thin silk or muslin and setting one end of it in a cardboard cylinder painted white, in which is fixed a light bulb. A flood of light within the column will be reflected when the lights are turned on. Various artistic lighting effects can also be obtained from the use of gauze or net. When lamps of high intensity are used for increased illumination, care should be exercised to avoid their contact with inflammable material.

THE LIGHT PLOT

After all plans for the lighting have been made and carried out, a smooth operation of the equipment will be assured only through the use of a "light" plot. This is a sheet which gives in detail every change in the stage lights and the cue on which each change is to occur. Although the electrician may have attended some of the general rehearsals previous to the dress rehearsal, the stage manager should have a separate light rehearsal at which time cues will be given and light changes made. Such a rehearsal, for example, will cause the stage to be lighted at the exact instant when a lantern on the stage is lit—not before and not after; it will insure a smooth operation of the lights throughout the production. Thus the stage manager will not only save much valuable time from the dress rehearsal, but he will also secure the most satisfactory lighting effects at the public performance.

CHAPTER XVII

THE STAGE PICTURE

The several scenes of the operetta are in reality a series of stage pictures by means of which the stage manager appeals to the eye of his audience. He will do well therefore to familiarize himself with the requisites of a good picture through a study of the reproductions of paintings in such magazines as *Mentor, Studio, National Geographic*, and *House and Garden*. In creating the various scene pictures the stage manager follows the rules of perspective, proportion, and balance that govern the artist who paints a picture on canvas, employing as his media of expression the scenery, the lighting, the costumes, the actors, and the properties.

PROPERTIES AND THEIR ARRANGEMENT

At the outset the stage manager will find that roughly drawn pencil sketches on which are marked the exact location of each object of his different scenes will be of great value, first, in making his picture, and later, as a guide to the property man. In locating the properties in his stage picture, the stage manager should see that the different objects bear the right relation to each other as well as to the stage as a whole,—experimentation on the stage itself being the best means of securing the most effective arrangement. He will remember too that very small articles, unless conspicuously placed, as on a mantel, are often lost to the view of the audience. On the other hand, large objects are quite often out of proportion, particularly in the foreground. This latter problem can be solved by building the necessary

163

PRACTICAL SETTING

(Colonial entrance, practical wall and arch with splendid detail)

windmill, tent, or gypsy wagon of a size which will be between the actual dimensions of the objects and the size suggested by rocks or trees in the backdrop. Similarly, the stage setting for a primary children's operetta should be suitably proportioned,—smaller than those used for an adult performance.

The arrangement of furniture and the use of floor space will likewise require consideration, particularly when the chorus is large and the stage is limited in size. When additional space is required in a particular scene, the stage manager may secure it by arranging for two minor characters to move a bench or a table to the side of, or off, the stage. He may have this done just prior to or during the entrance of the chorus. As he distributes the properties in his stage picture, the stage manager should remember, however, that the audience is interested primarily in the actors themselves; as he locates the properties, therefore, he will keep in mind the characters of his ever-changing picture, particularly the large groups to be used in the finales.

INTEREST AND BALANCE

Two important elements which characterize every effective stage picture and which should constantly be kept in mind by the stage manager are the center of interest and balance. These two elements are interrelated and indispensable. As in every painting there is a center of interest which attracts the eye, so in the correct stage picture the various details are so arranged that the attention is drawn to and held by a figure, an action, or an effect. This center of interest must never be obscured. To illustrate, in the Richmond hiring fair scene from the opera *Martha* by Flotow, the peasants and servants are scattered about the stage, distributed some at the left, some at the right, and some in the center back. They chat and saunter about, occasionally directing their glances and action to the sheriff, whose hat, wig, and cane come in for attention.   Later they press closely about him in an annoying fashion, but in such a manner as never to obscure this officer of the law from the view of the audience.   Soon the farmers who have come to hire, standing, now with one servant, now with another, form, with the sheriff, the center of interest.   From time to time this center of interest shifts about the stage but never is the view of the audience obstructed.   In his plans for the

JOB AND HIS COMFORTERS
(Dignified simplicity of setting with perfect grouping)
Stuart Walker's production of *The Book of Job*

arrangement of people on the stage, the stage manager will find helpful suggestions among the illustrations in such dramatic magazines as the *Drama* or the *Theater*.

THE ACTORS IN THE PICTURE

Professional actors never step out of the frame formed by the proscenium arch, nor should the amateur, with a possible exception or two. For instance, in a primary oper-etta, when a childish voice fails to carry in an auditorium which has imperfect acoustics, the director may have the singer step down to the footlights for his solos. Otherwise, all actors should remain back of the proscenium arch.

THE MOVEMENT OF ACTORS

Whether there be few or many persons on the stage, the stage manager should move them about according to the demands of the dialogue and the action of the scene in such a manner that due prominence will be given to the out-standing characters of the moment, that no individual will be hidden behind another, and that the proper relationship between the actors themselves and the stage picture as a whole will be maintained. At all times he should direct the movements of his actors so as to maintain the two elements just mentioned—interest and balance. He will accomplish this objective best through the use of that device which is known as the "stage cross"—a device which he should study in detail.

THE STAGE CROSS

Two characters, *A* and *B*, are on the stage. *A* stands on the left as they face the audience, *B* on the right. *A* speaks: "I will leave these papers with you and be on my way." As he speaks, *A* crosses to the right and with his right hand gives the papers mentioned to *B*, who moves toward *A* to receive them in his left hand: passing in front of *B*, *A* exits at the right. After he has received the papers, *B* takes two or three steps toward the left in order to preserve the balance of the stage picture. It should be observed that the domi-nant character of the moment always crosses in front,—in this instance it is *A*. His face should be turned slightly toward the audience in order that his lines may be heard. Had *B* failed to move in the opposite direction when *A* moved, he would for the moment have been half concealed behind *A*. He would, moreover, have interfered with *A's* exit, and thereby have committed that stage offense which is known as "hogging the stage." This uncomplimentary term is applied to any actor who interferes with or detracts from the action of the character who is dominant at the moment—thus diverting the attention of the audience from the actor who should be the center of interest. If there are on the stage characters who are silent during a dialogue which demands a cross, the stage manager should see to it that these persons also keep the scene in balance. To maintain this balance it may be necessary for them to cross unobstrusively; but they should always cross "in character" and behind those players who are, for the moment, the center of interest. The following diagram is an illustration of the stage cross described above:

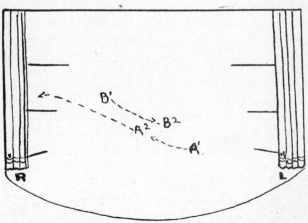

A more complex cross, or series of crosses will be understood by the following illustration from *The Chimes o*,

Normandy.   Act **II** is laid in the Hunting Hall of an old
Chateau, supposedly haunted, into which three characters
—Serpolette, Grenicheux, and Bailli (the sheriff)—enter.
Groping they assume these positions:

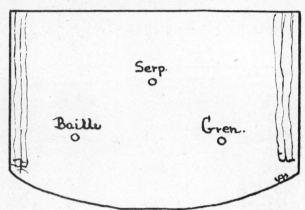

Suddenly they are surprised by the entrance of a group of
people composed of Henri, the real owner of the chateau,
and Germaine, the lost marchioness, accompanied by retainers and peasants   They then assume this grouping:

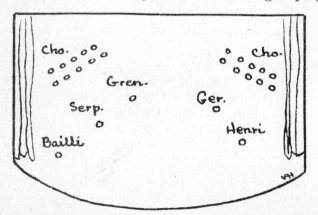

The important dialogue which is soon to occur between

Bailli and Henri and which in turn is to be followed by a
solo by the former, requires that these two, Henri and Bailli,
have the center of the stage. To this end, Henri crosses
Germaine, and the Bailli crosses Serpolette and Grenicheux.

During the opening lines of the dialogue, Serpolette
crosses Grenicheux and the stage picture as to characters is
as follows:

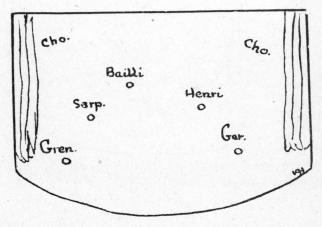

This grouping prepares for the action which is soon to
occur, when Serpolette and Germaine are to move back in
order to examine objects in front of which they are now
standing.

The diagonal lines in which the chorus is thus grouped
not only economize stage space and permit free action on
the part of the principals, but also allow an unobstructed
view of the up-stage with its suits of armor, where the
interest of the audience is centered as the scene moves to
its climax. This arrangement therefore meets the demands
of balance and center of interest.

An excellent example of conformity to these two essentials
in the stage picture is to be found in the opening scenes of
Act I in the opera *Martha*. On the left of the stage, a

viewed by the audience, is Lady Harriet, maid of honor to the queen, seated before her dressing table.   At her side is her maid, Nancy, assisting in the finishing touches of her mistress' toilet.   On the stage at the right are grouped the ladies in attendance, who, in an opening chorus, sing the

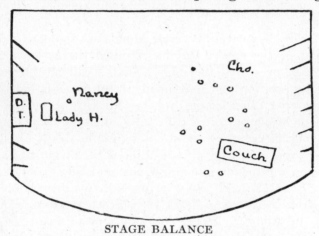

STAGE BALANCE

charms of Lady Harriet.   In this instance the center of interest, Lady Harriet, soon to be wooed by the elderly beau, Sir Tristam, is unobscured, and the proper balance in the scene is cleverly secured.

The preceding discussion and examples emphasize the necessity of thought and study in the arrangement of properties and in the movement of actors.

THE STAGE MANAGER'S PROCEDURE

Good stage pictures do not just happen!   They come about only as a result of definite plans which have been made in advance and carefully followed out.   The stage manager, pressed for time, is often tempted to disregard this fact and to rely, at rehearsals, upon the inspiration of the moment from which to determine the stage business of a scene.   Such a procedure, however, is quite likely to result in plans that are indefinite and incomplete—in the omission of certain action or groupings, which, had they been included, would have added much to the effectiveness of the production. Moreover, experience proves that such an eleventh hour method actually requires much more of the actor's and the stage manager's time than when rehearsals are definitely planned.

After he has carefully read aloud the spoken lines and the text of the music, and has studied the action and the scene to be presented, the stage manager will carefully determine the position and movement of the various individuals and groups. In working out for himself, scene by scene, the stage business, as it is called, the amateur stage manager will avoid haphazard dramatic action if he draws a diagram of the stage, indicating the position of the larger properties, and showing the various positions and movements of the different actors. He may represent furniture and large properties by "oblongs," the players by "crosses," and the chorus by "dots." As the characters move about the stage in keeping with the dialogue and the spirit of the scene, he should draw fresh diagrams to indicate the new positions of each actor and the chorus. Besides helping him in his preparation for the first presentation of the operetta, the various diagrams and suggestions will aid the stage manager in future performances of this same operetta, and will also be of service to him as a guide in formulating the stage business for other operettas he may later present.

Having located the properties and having made definite plans for the stage business, the stage manager, or preferably an assistant, should, during each rehearsal, make copious notes of any changes or additions which he wishes to incorporate. In this connection, George Bernard Shaw, who has been called the greatest living stage director, says: "The first time I ever counted my notes was when I had to produce *Arms and the Man* in ten rehearsals. The total was six hundred. That is a minimum; I have run into thousands since."

ASSISTANT STAGE MANAGER

When a large and pretentious school operetta is to be given, or when groups from various schools join in giving a production, the stage manager will find it advisable to avail himself of the help of an assistant stage manager. This person may be a faculty member, but in the smaller schools an upperclassman who has had experience in dramatic production may also be a desirable choice.

The assistant stage manager should attend all rehearsals. With pencil and prompt copy in hand, he should sit beside the stage manager and take notes on changes or minor corrections which need to be given attention after the rehearsal. Such an arrangement saves holding up all the performers for each bit of correction. For illustration: a certain character engaged in dialogue is holding a book in his right hand. The stage manager decides that it will be more effective for him to hold it in the left hand. Instead of interrupting the action, he asks the assistant to make a note: *A* should hold book in left hand. Thus he economizes time and does not interfere with the dialogue and movement of the scene which is being rehearsed.

THE STAGE MANAGER'S GUIDE

The presentation of an operetta is made much easier and far more effective if a stage manager's guide is used. Such a guide, or *prompt copy* as it is sometimes called, is an interleaved copy of the score, containing for each scene drawings for the stage setting, descriptions of the costumes, and explicit directions for entrances, exits, groupings, individual and group action, and pantomime. A light-plot and property-plot for each scene are also included. For the amateur producer, such a guide does several things. It places before him the stage setting and action of each scene of the production. At the same time it familiarizes him with the technique of stage production. Since such technique is carefully studied by every professional producer, it is interesting to speculate why the amateur has ignored it. No one ever acquires the ability to play the piano correctly without a knowledge of the technique; no more can one dispense with the knowledge of stage production. Furthermore, a stage guide enables a stage manager to delegate to assistants much work, that, were it not explicitly mapped out, he himself would be compelled to do. For instance, after going over the guide with an assistant he may turn over to him the rehearsal of a particular scene, knowing that nothing will have to be undone. Again, the use of a prompt copy will secure equal emphasis upon all phases of a production, and a chorus action which will be uniform and exactly timed.

PROFESSIONAL STAGE GUIDES

Stage manager's guides compiled by professionals may be rented from houses specializing in stage material. The comic operas of Gilbert and Sullivan, the light operas of Victor Herbert, and many of the recent musical comedies are presented in a form that has become accepted, and for the most part so definitely fixed as to be considered standardized. The rental cost of these stage guides is approximately ten dollars for a period of from thirty to sixty days. A royalty of from $50 to $150 must be paid for the privilege of producing a light opera or a musical comedy on which the copyright has not expired.

MAKING A STAGE GUIDE

In staging the average school operetta for which no prompt copy is available, the stage manager will find it advisable to construct his own prompt copy. He should first interleave a copy of the operetta with blank pages. At the beginning of each scene he should make a sketch of the stage setting and the position of the larger stage properties. He should next cut up two copies of the libretto, which is usually published separately from the score. He should then paste the various speeches of the dialogue on the blank pages directly opposite the music numbers between which they occur. A few school operettas are accompanied by pamphlets which give some suggestions for dramatic action; these also will be more valuable and convenient if they are transferred to the pages of the prompt copy. On the page opposite a chorus or a solo, he should draw diagrams illustrating the action of both the chorus and the principals which he wishes to apply to the music and words on the opposite page. He should then select a certain word on which each action will start and finish, and mark this word with some sign. If music accompanies the speech, he should mark the exact measure of the music with the same sign. For the conductor as he directs in front of the stage, this interleaved copy is most valuable during the rehearsals and the final performance; one glance at it will show him exactly what should be taking place upon the stage.

The specific directions which have to do with the dramatic action will be the most numerous. They should include not only definite instructions as to the movement and action of groups, but of individuals as well. No feature of the stage business should be considered too insignificant for attention. For example, the action and position of the soloists should not always be down-center. The reader can doubtless recall numerous examples when a young amateur has gone through his part of the action creditably enough up to the time for his solo, only to drop out of character with his introduction music, step deliberately toward the footlights, fold his hands in a sophisticated recital manner, and begin his song. For such a stilted procedure, not the singer but the director is responsible. Studying a scene, with pencil in hand, the stage manager will discover that some soloists may be placed down-left, others down-right, and occasionally some in an up-stage position. A slight change of position during the singing of a verse is often very desirable. In any event the actor should take a few steps and slightly alter his position during the interlude. Futhermore, the stage manager must work out the gestures to be employed during the soloist's singing. In the average production, solos are noticeably weak, from a dramatic standpoint. Explicit instructions for the action of soloists are rarely included in prompt copies. This is true not only of the well-known light operas, but also of the school operetta. If the solos therefore are to be anything more than a mere singing of words, the stage manager should go through them beforehand and indicate such specific gestures and movements as will add emphasis and interest.

A stage manager's guide for any school operetta may usually be secured from the publisher, with the libretto.

STAGE TERMINOLOGY

For the benefit of those who may be unfamiliar with stage phraseology of a professional prompt copy, the following explanations are made. Stage directions are always given from the actor's position on the stage as he faces the audience. The right wing, therefore, is the left as viewed from the audience. The floor of the professional stage was formerly slightly higher toward the back; hence "up-stage" means to the back of the stage, and "down-stage" means toward the front; C means center; L. C. means left center; R.C. means right center; L-1, L-2, L-3, mean first left entrance, second left entrance, and third left entrance; R-1, R-2, R-3 mean first right entrance, second right entrance, and third right entrance. Other stage locations and entrances are distinguished as follows:

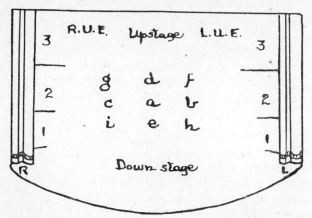

1. RIGHT FIRST ENTRANCE
2. RIGHT SECOND ENTRANCE
3. RIGHT THIRD ENTRANCE
   OR UPPER ENTRANCE
a. CENTER
b. LEFT CENTER

c. RIGHT CENTER
d. CENTER BACK
e. DOWN FRONT
f. BACK LEFT
g. BACK RIGHT
h. DOWN LEFT
i. DOWN RIGHT

USING THE GUIDE

After having determined upon his stage pictures and the dramatic action for each act, and having indicated these in the prompt copy, the stage manager must repeatedly go over this action until it is thoroughly fixed in his memory. Before each rehearsal he should have definitely in mind what each character is to do. This advance preparation on the part of the stage manager will be found to be both effective and economical. It is quite as necessary that the stage manager and the chorus members should know exactly what they are to *do* during every moment of the scene as it is for them to know their words and music. The stage manager who must stop to consult his prompt copy each time before he gives a direction for stage action will lose the attention of the young actors, just as the actor who pauses to refresh his memory from the libretto interrupts the movement of the dialogue. Only when he is thoroughly familiar in advance with his prompt copy will the stage manager inspire that confidence in the cast and chorus which will awaken dramatic response, and put life, or "pep" into the production. Obviously, then, the far-sighted stage manager will not only provide himself with a guide, or prompt copy, but he will freely interleave it, thoroughly *study* it, and constantly use it.

Enough has been said to make plain that only when the stage manager prepares carefully in advance, arranging his stage properties with perspective in mind and moving the actors in a manner which will maintain balance and center of interest; only when he takes time to make ample notes in his prompt copy and to fix these details clearly in his own mind before his rehearsals, will it be possible for him to give to the stage picture the desired illusion of reality and to move definitely toward the one goal—a successful public performance.

CHAPTER XVIII

STAGE EFFECTS

Since the operetta is a make-believe experience, whatever will aid in creating a sense of reality should be utilized. Scenery, costumes, action, the lines of the actors, and the lighting,—all contribute to this end. There is still another means, however, which the stage manager may employ in producing the illusion of reality, namely, the "mechanical" or "stage" effects, such as a flash of lightning, the tolling of a distant bell, or the pungent odor of incense. Since such devices appeal to the ears or the eyes of the audience at a moment when their imagination is alert, they give that much desired impression of actuality that pervades a scene and persists long after the production has become a memory. The chiming of the castle clock in *The Chimes of Normandy* or the glowing fire from the forge of the gypsy camp in *Il Trovatore* produce an atmosphere that goes far in creating a sense of reality and in holding the interest of an audience.

SOUNDS

HORSES' HOOFS

The sound of horses' hoofs is produced by striking together the two halves of a dry cocoanut shell. The roll of carriage wheels is imitated by pushing or dragging a long pole across the stage floor.

STEAM ENGINE

A puffing steam engine is suggested by rubbing together

two 3 x 6 wooden blocks, the inner surfaces of which are covered with coarse sand paper.

EXPLOSIONS

An explosion or a cannonade is produced by striking the head of a bass drum, which is well tightened.

RIFLE SHOTS

A volley of rifle shots is imitated by whipping rattans on a dried calf-skin. If a loosened bass drum head is beaten with light dowel strips, obtainable from the manual training department, a similar effect will be produced.

THUNDER

Thunder can be realistically counterfeited by rolling a twelve or sixteen pound shot, or a bowling ball, down a narrow trough made of wood, on the bottom of which have been nailed wooden cleats. Another simple device for imitating the sound of thunder, and one which is more often employed, is that of striking a suspended piece of sheet iron or heavy tin with a wooden mallet and allowing the iron to swing back and forth as it reverberates.

CRASH OF DISHES

The effect of an off-stage crash of dishes is secured by letting fall a basket of broken crockery and glassware, or by dropping two large tin trays that are piled one upon the other.

WIND

Wind in all degrees, from the gentle breeze to the shriek of the hurricane, is "made" with startling effect by the following device: On a cylinder is stretched canvas, or old silk.

Within this cylinder is rotated by a handle an axle or a wooden drum. To this drum or axle are fastened thin

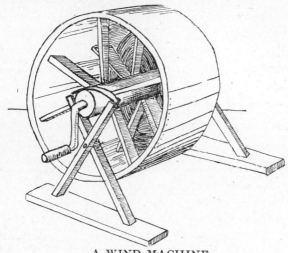

A WIND MACHINE

wooden strips or spokes, the ends of which rub against the canvas as the handle is turned.

BELLS

Bell sounds in their wide variety cannot be produced by a mere desk bell or a cow bell. A little gong, a bar of steel, an axle, or a suspended brake drum from an automobile will imitate the effect of chimes and large bells. To simulate the sound of a ship's bell or an old-fashioned hall clock, a triangle, not too small, is used.

HORNS

A hunting horn is best imitated by a muted cornet or horn played off-stage. Occasionally a scene will require a chime of a definite pitch, as for example in *Il Trovatore* or *The Chimes of Normandy*. Such a pitch will be obtained by taking a piece of bar steel, the pitch of which is slightly lower than that desired, and shortening the bar to a length which will give the correct number of vibrations. The preparation of this and similar mechanisms will serve as a fine project for the science department.

TOM-TOMS

The monotonous sound of a tom-tom for an Indian scene is made by beating with a soft hammer upon a small side drum, the head of which has been loosened. An art-gum eraser, with an improvised handle, will serve as a soft hammer.

ANIMAL SOUNDS

Various off-stage sounds, such as bird calls, animal sounds, etc., may be obtained by playing carefully selected and properly manipulated phonograph records. The ocarina, or a similar toy, may also be used effectively in reproducing bird calls.

WHISTLES

The whistle of a steam-boat or of an engine is simulated by blowing across the upper edge of a glass or brass tube, the lower end of which is closed.

WAVES, WATERFALLS, AND RAIN

The sound of ocean waves is imitated by rolling back and forth a cheese box or a bass drum containing small pebbles, peas, or shelled corn. To produce the noise of a water-fall, the box or drum should be filled to only one-eighth of its capacity and rolled continuously. The sound of rain is simulated by beating a wire brush lightly on the head of a snare drum.

PISTOL SHOTS

The firing of a pistol, when required, should be entrusted to a careful adult who is provided with *blank* cartridges.

An undesirable echo will be avoided if the shot is fired out of a door which opens off the stage. As with other startling effects, so with shooting, "a little goes a long way." In fact, when any stage effect is overdone the result is apt to be that of a melodramatic atmosphere.

TIMING OF SOUNDS

Mob-cries, laughter, and singing off-stage should be carefully rehearsed in order that the proper volume may be secured; a leader should be appointed who will take the responsibilities for cues and for indicating the length of time the sound is to continue. An ill-timed peal of thunder that covers a dialogue, or an explosion that occurs too late, creates, not the effect of realism, but that of burlesque.

VISUAL EFFECTS

SNOWFALL AND RAIN

To imitate a realistic snow-fall, a small amount of powdered mica mixed with finely cut squares of white tissue paper or white confetti should be equally distributed in a trough suspended above the stage, so that when the trough is rocked back and forth the snow will fall in a realistic manner. An electric fan, properly located in relation to the trough, will add realism to a snow scene. Snow on the hats or clothing of characters who enter from without is simulated by the use of slightly moistened salt.

In an outdoor scene, the effect of falling rain is produced by dropping rice from above the stage upon a grass carpet. In an indoor scene—a scene in which the audience is looking through a stage window at a storm outside—the appearance of rain is given by vibrating finely polished wires which are suspended vertically, or by dropping rice from above upon a canvas back of the window. The rice falling upon the canvas adds to the illusion the sound of falling rain.   In each case the effect is more realistic if a light is played on the wires or on the falling rice.

LIGHTNING

Lightning is produced by igniting photographic "flash" powder or magnesium, or by flashing on an off green electric lights.   A more realistic effect is obtained by attaching the two wires of an electric circuit, preferably that of an electric battery, to a coarse file or rasp and to a carbon. By touching the carbon on the file a flash is made; and by drawing the carbon along the surface of the file a most vivid pyrotechnic display is produced.   A green gelatine placed between the device and the audience intensifies the effect.   Care should be exercised in the use of this device to prevent the operator from receiving an electric shock.

A mechanical device which contributes much to the illusion of reality in a gypsy or rural scene is that of the blacksmith's anvil.   In a setting where such an anvil is included an atmosphere of "sparkling" reality is added if the anvil and hammer are wired in an electric battery circuit which is opened and closed as the hammer strikes the anvil— thereby producing convincing sparks at each stroke.

MOONLIGHT

An illusion of moonlight is obtained from using light bulbs colored light blue, or from causing a bunch light to shine through a blue sheet of gelatine.

CRESCENT MOON

The effect of a crescent moon may be produced by constructing a paper box in the front of which is cut a crescent.   Inside the box is placed an electric bulb, and the box is suspended by cords.   The device is hung back of a scrim curtain or low border painted to match the section of the

scene in which the moon is to be used. The appearance of
a rising moon may be obtained by slowly raising the moon

device behind a woodwing covered with scrim which has been
painted to correspond to the other woodwings.

FIRE, DAWN, SUNSET

Fire, dawn, and sunset are simulated by the use of red lights.

SMOKE

Smoke is most safely produced by using a "smoke pot," which is purchasable from any dealer in fire-works or through the chemistry department.

ALCOHOLIC BEVERAGES

Alcoholic beverages are represented best by tea.

WATER

By the use of a moving picture machine, the waves of a lake or of the ocean may be quite naturally reproduced on the backdrop.

CLOUDS

A most vivid effect of moving clouds is created by stitching together several widths of muslin, painting or dyeing them sky blue, and then painting on this background different cloud effects.   By winding this painted muslin on rollers which are set vertically at angles on each side of the stage and by unwinding it from one roller to the other across the stage a realistic effect is obtained.

SHIP SILHOUETTES

The silhouette of a ship on the horizon may be made by cutting the ship's outline from beaver board.   Flash lights or incandescent lamps set behind small holes which have been cut in this outline will produce a realistic scene on a darkened stage.

SUPERNATURAL EFFECTS

Phosphorescent paint on the face and costume of an actor gives a supernatural effect.

Small green bulbs wired to a dry battery which is hidden in an actor's costume will add thrills to a witching hour. Employing a similar device the eyes of frogs and other stage animals can be made to blink and shine by flashing the electric current off and on.

ODORS

Odors, such as incense used in oriental scenes, characteristic perfumes, the aroma of boiling coffee, and the odor of smoking tobacco, appeal to a third sense, and help to create the desired illusion.

In the employment of stage effects the stage manager will do well to remember that simple devices are the most dependable, and that careful rehearsals should be held if such are to be used. As has been said, mechanical effects have a place only in certain operettas. To many a production, however, an ingenious stage carpenter or clever electrician may, by the introduction of a simple mechanical device, add a touch of realism not otherwise obtainable.

CHAPTER XIX

Business Detail

The business manager, the general director, and all associated in the preparation of the operetta will of course have as their first aim an artistic production. Second in their consideration will be the financial success of the performance. An excellent operetta which achieves artistic success may easily fail from the standpoint of finance. So sure of the real worth of the performance are the producer and those associated in the production that they often take for granted a large audience and an ample profit.

It is obvious that the expenditure of money in connection with an operetta must be very carefully supervised. Whatever expense is required to make the production artistic and in every way complete, is justifiable. Too great freedom in expenditure, however, may convert a possible profit into a loss. Purchases should not be made indiscriminately by assistants; anything which must be contracted for should be bought only with the approval of the director and the business manager. With the assistance of the supervisor or the director in charge, the business manager will be wise if he works out, at the first, a budget which will distribute the items of expense and secure a satisfactory net return.

IMPORTANT FACTORS

Several factors enter into the successful business management of an operetta. These may be summed up under the heads of general publicity and advertising, ticket selling campaign, and control of expenditures. Before the date of the operetta is announced, careful inquiry should be made as to all entertainments which have already been scheduled or which are under consideration. As soon as the date of the performance is definitely settled, it should be publicly announced in order to avoid conflict with other entertainments which may be scheduled. The first announcement may be given advertising value by playing upon the curiosity of the public; for instance, a front page notice—"You have an engagement for June 1st," or "Reserve June 1st" printed on stickers to be used on automobiles and other places where permissible—are good publicity technique. Such advertising will arouse curiosity and will help to keep alive interest in the operetta until its performance. It is not enough, however, to announce the date. Hopeful producers often close their eyes, see a packed house, and a "standing room only" sign. The business manager and his associates should remember that for every half dollar which a prospective ticket-purchaser may spend to see the operetta, there are half-a-dozen items for which this same piece of money may be expended—movies, small luxuries, or even necessary articles! It is a fine psychological task therefore to induce the possessor of that half dollar to prefer the operetta to any of these other things.

ADVERTISING

The local small town editor, with whom the director, if wise, has long been well acquainted, will be glad to use a limited amount of material that has news value. Paid advertising, however, should not be overlooked, not only because it has value in itself but also because it establishes contact with the local press. Such advertising will serve several purposes: it will remind people to keep the date free from other social engagements, it will reach transient ticket purchasers and people in neighboring communities, and it will give a semiprofessional character to the performance. The type of such advertising will depend somewhat upon the size of the town or city. If a display advertisement is taken, a good location should be requested, as for example a space following the "personals," one on the editorial page, or one on the back page.   In a city, front page "readers" are the most profitable form of advertising, because they briefly but pointedly keep before the public the operetta performance, its date, and the price of tickets.   Moreover,

LIVE ADVERTISING

paid advertising is often an effective means of opening the columns of the paper to items and news stories relating to the operetta.   The publishing of such articles will mean, of course, that some one connected with the preparation of the operetta must carefully search out items of interest which may serve as the basis for news stories.   A complete story containing all details in the first announcement defeats its own end; interest will be aroused by such a method, but not maintained.   As previously suggested, the English department, through its newspaper English classes, may be of great assistance in this sort of advertising.   Frequently in a small town or city, arrangement can be made with the local telephone company for advertising; during hours when the lines are not very busy, operators will call a selected list of rural subscribers to remind them of the operetta and the ticket sale. Another effective means of advertising a grade operetta is that of presenting certain numbers, or perhaps even an entire scene in costume at the senior high chapel. Again, the manager of the local moving picture theater will usually consent to run a slide containing an announcement of the operetta, presupposing, of course, that he has been consulted before the date of the operetta was announced. Even more effective advertising, and advertising which is worth any reasonable expenditure, is that of running a slide made from a photograph of a scene or of some of the cast in costume. In short, clever and continuous advertising will do much to insure the financial success of the operetta.

PRICE OF TICKETS

The price and sale of tickets is another matter which should be given careful consideration. An ideal plan is to admit by complimentary tickets the sponsoring society and the school community—the latter including the parents of the school children, the school board, etc. Obviously, such an arrangement is possible only when expenses are cared for by some existing fund other than the music fund. In a forward-looking community which expends a given amount annually on an "Entertainment Course," the operetta is paid for as a regular number of the course and the patrons are admitted on their season tickets. When, as is usual, there is to be an admission price, it should be fixed so that it will not be too high to preclude a capacity house, or too low to cover expenses. Occasionally a matinee performance is held for children at a minimum price, on the day preceding the final performance. The night performance is then given at a single admission price for adults. In a small town the price scale ranges from twenty-five to fifty cents. To price tickets above the customary charge for similar events is a doubtful procedure. A popular price is much more likely to insure a packed house. A skillful "scaling" of ticket prices will often result in a higher net return. A few of the more desirable seats may be priced above the rest. In a large auditorium a scale of three prices may be practical. Such an arrangement induces the early purchase of tickets by those who wish the choice seats. If all the lower-priced seats are sold before the night of the performance, late comers may still buy tickets in this higher-priced section. The plan of selling a section of the house to purchasers of reserved seats often stimulates the advanced sale. If one-half of the number of seats in the auditorium can be sold in advance, the regular box office sale should insure a capacity house.

PATRONS AND PATRONESSESS

The selection of a list of twelve to fifty prominent people as patrons and patronesses, each influential in his own group, will give "tone" to a performance, as well as aid materially the ticket sale, particularly in a small city. Sometimes these patrons and patronesses will become responsible for a given number of tickets. Again, in the case of an unusually elaborate production, they may sign a guarantee fund against a deficit. Occasionally these persons will allow their names to be used in advance notices and on the programs as sponsors.

SELLING THE TICKETS

The business manager will be wise to inaugurate early a ticket-selling campaign. An effective scheme is that of allowing a pass, rather than a ticket, to each person selling a given number of tickets. If people are given an opportunity to make reservations by mail before the sale of seats is thrown open to the general public, not only will tickets be sold but interest in the coming performance will be stimulated. Since every audience includes many who have bough tickets simply because someone else has done so, an advance sale of tickets to influencial people is a most valuable means of advertising. Members of the cast and chorus are often the best medium for selling tickets. Occasionally a class or an organization will sponsor a ticket selling campaign for a small percentage of the net profit after expenses have been paid. Under any circumstances, the business manager should keep in close contact with the ticket sale so that he may keep himself informed as to any advertising that may be required, and so that he may give attention to any groups or individuals selling tickets who may need suggestions or assistance.

HIRING THE HALL

If the operetta is to be given in an auditorium other than the school auditorium or the regular headquarters of an amateur organization, very definite arrangements should be made beforehand as to stage help, additional musicians who will be needed, lighting equipment, and any extras for which a bill might afterwards be rendered. If the local theater is rented for a performance, the contract should release the organization from liability of every sort.

PROGRAM

Program copy should be furnished the business manager for printing, which will include the customary information of date, time, and place. A frequent omission is that of the name of the city. The director should make sure that the program includes the names of all members of the cast and chorus, the assistants and aides, together with the proper acknowledgment of any special courtesies. The proof should be read carefully by two persons, attention being given to the spelling of names.

THE PROCEEDS

At this point a pertinent query is, "What shall be done

with the proceeds?" This question is one which should be considered before the performance—in fact early in the formulation of the plans. Failure to settle this point at the beginning has sometimes led to misunderstandings among those who have staged an amateur performance. Again, an indefinite answer to this question has frequently resulted in keen disappointment to a group who have put on a school operetta with the idea that the proceeds were to be turned over to the music fund or some allied fund, only to find in the end that the money has been diverted to the athletic fund or some general fund equally unconnected with the giving of the operetta. The early announcement of a specific purpose to which the net returns from the operetta will be devoted is not only an excellent incentive but it is an aid in advertising. If there exists in the school some such need as music equipment, for which school funds are positively unavailable, this need will furnish an excellent objective. Again, since the ideal and most successful production is the result of a cooperative effort of departments, the expenditure of the profit from the operetta upon a work of art which will be enjoyed by the entire school will meet the approval of everyone. For example, one school has purchased from the proceeds of its grade operettas a radio, an orthophonic victrola, several worth-while bronze statues, and a series of reproductions of Abbey's *Quest of the Holy Grail*—a frieze in the public library of Boston.

Although the financial returns do not place the final stamp of value on an operetta, there is no reason why it should not be an accompanying part of a successful production. When preparatory expenditures have been carefully made, when tactful and effective advertising has been done, and when methodized salesmanship of tickets has been properly supervised, there remains no reason why the operetta should not be financially successful.

CHAPTER XX

The Dress Rehearsal and Final Performance

THE DRESS REHEARSAL

Prior to the dress rehearsal the director should have held relatively short rehearsals; however, if he be wise, he will allow plenty of time for this final rehearsal. If costumes are ready for use and all other arrangements have been completed, and ideal plan is to hold the dress rehearsal two days before the final performance. It should be called for an early hour, the chorus assembling first for their make-up and then the principals for theirs. If the operetta is being given by children of the primary and intermediate grades, a daylight rehearsal may be possible—provided that the lighting effects and the make-up have been tried out on a previous evening.

When possible, the chorus should come to the auditorium costumed. If this cannot be arranged, ample dressing room facilities should be provided for them with responsible assistants at hand.

This final rehearsal should be a replica, in advance, of the final performance; no detail should be omitted. Make-up, costumes, scenery, action, and lighting,—all should be exactly as they will be at the final performance. The rehearsal should be marked by completeness as to detail, by the absence of eleventh hour changes, and perhaps more than anything else, by patience and an entire elimination of "nerves."

Whereas some directors of experience believe that a small group of sympathetic listeners accustoms the cast and the chorus to the "feel" of an audience, the young and inexperienced director will do well to refuse admittance to any persons other than those assistants who may be able to offer helpful suggestions.

It should be made clear to all members of the cast and chorus that no friends or relatives will be permitted behind the scenes on the night of the operetta.   At the call of the stage manager, before the overture is begun and before the rise of the first curtain, every one must be in his place on the stage.   After this no one will be permitted to leave the stage until the rise of the curtain.

Members should be coached on holding their action or delaying their dialogue until the applause or laughter in the audience has ceased, and upon continuing their parts at a signal from the conductor.   Encores, too, should be rehearsed; the singers should understand just what numbers or parts of numbers *may* be repeated, and the definite places of beginning and ending them.   Only short encores should be included in the average operetta and if any of these are likely to occur at the close of a scene, the curtain man should be advised as to exactly what will be expected of him.   Principals and those in the front row of the chorus should become accustomed to the curtain line.   It may be wise to indicate this line on the stage floor by chalk marks, so that every performer may make sure, just before the curtain is to fall, that he is back of the curtain line,—without looking up to see where the curtain is!   When the curtain is lowered the cast and chorus should hold their positions; at a signal from the stage manager all players should leave the stage *immediately*, the principals and chorus going to their assigned rooms, with instructions to remain there until they are called.

SAVING TIME

Since it is unlikely that the final performance will move much more rapidly than does the dress rehearsal, the stage manager will at this rehearsal note carefully all places in the performance where time may be economized. He should observe and remedy any details in the scene shifting; he should discover and arrange to give assistance to those actors who are apt not to be costumed in ample time for the succeeding act; he should impress upon the stage crew, the cast, and the entire chorus that they will individually contribute to the success of the performance by knowing the precise location of all of those things for which they are responsible,—the exact place where they will find definite pieces of scenery, certain properties, their dressing rooms, the smaller parts of their costumes, etc.

Time will pass much more quickly and pleasantly for the audience while the scenery is being shifted and costumes changed if the orchestra or accompanist plays between acts. It will add interest if numbers are selected which will exactly fill the time required, these numbers being announced as a special feature at the bottom of the program. If local conditions seem to necessitate a wait of more than six or eight minutes between acts, an entr'acte may be introduced before the curtain. Such an act should be used only when absolutely necessary, and should be of a type that will not interrupt the continuity of the performance any more than can be helped; of course, to some seasoned opera goers even the ballet is an interruption. Under no circumstances should anything be introduced between acts which will occupy more than the time actually required for the changing of scenery and costumes.

CUE SHEETS

The stage manager will find the use of cue sheets an invaluable aid in securing prompt entrances both of chorus and principals. These cue sheets, prepared in advance, one for each act, should be fastened on the walls of the dressing rooms as well as in a place convenient to the entrances.

There should be a copy of the entrance cues taken from the stage manager's guide; for example: Act I, Scene I, Chorus of Peasants—to left upper entrance during the Count's solo. Get-ready cue, "The haughty one." Entrance cue, "From every land." Scene II, "Queen of the Fairies"—*ready* to enter, at first lower entrance right at beginning of the Chorus of Elves; entrance cue—closing words, "We serve the Fairy Queen." Just before the close of Act I, the cue sheets for Act I should be removed and those for Act II should be posted. The inexperienced director may not understand the importance of these cue sheets; the director who has "aged years" while waiting for a belated entrance of a chorus or principal will appreciate their value. Next to a quick change of scenery, nothing will contribute more toward an early final curtain that the use of detailed and accurate cue sheets.

THE PROMPTING

An ideal plan is to announce early that there will be no regular prompter and to insist upon the young actors being responsible for their own lines. The safer procedure, however, is to locate in the wings a prompter,—a dependable person who is thoroughly familiar with the production and who has carefully followed it through one full rehearsal before the dress rehearsal. This individual should have no other responsibilities connected with the operetta. Although his location may be known to the actors, they should be charged that under no circumstances should they turn toward him. His work as prompter will, of course, be facilitated by the use of a stage guide. In small amateur productions or high school operettas where the director is also the stage manager, and where he conducts the entire performance from the pit in front of the stage, he will find that he himself can best take care of the prompting. The members of the chorus should be assigned a definite place where

they are to remain between acts, for a quiet chorus behind
scenes, which keeps away from exits and entrances, is a joy!
Quick changes of costumes by the principal characters will
be possible if temporary dressing rooms are arranged; such
a place may be made by hanging a curtain across a corner
of the stage just behind the scenes.

RESULTS OF THE DRESS REHEARSAL

The dress rehearsal will have served its purpose when it
has accustomed the characters to their costumes, when it has
fixed cues definitely in the minds of all, including the off-
stage assistants, when it has revealed to the director the slow
spots in the action, and finally, when it has created the atmosphere of the operetta itself and has given to all performers inspiration and a desire for the final performance.
Even when conscientious work has been done at rehearsals,
even when details have been carefully considered and responsibility definitely assumed by proper assistants, the director
should not be discouraged if the dress rehearsal fails in some
particulars to have the desired movement and finish.   It is
a stage maxim that "A poor dress rehearsal augurs a good
public performance."   The director should dismiss rehearsal
as early as possible, with a few words of caution and many
of encouragement.   Everyone will return then for the final
performance with a desire to do his best, fully determined
that any slight mistakes which may have occurred during
the rehearsal shall not recur at the final performance.

THE FINAL PERFORMANCE

If the dress rehearsal has been complete in every detail, the
public performance will then consist merely of a repetition
of that rehearsal, plus the added inspiration of the audience.
When all preparatory details have been adequately cared
for, no strenuous duties will burden the performers on the

day of the performance; all should have some opportunity for rest. The conductor himself should not fail to take time for relaxation, for his mental attitude will be reflected in the people on the stage throughout the entire production.

Fully half an hour before time for the curtain to rise, the work of making up the chorus and the principals should be completed. If the other details are likewise given early attention, there will be established that feeling of readiness and composure which are essential for a successful production. Public announcement that the overture will begin promptly at an early hour, provision for plenty of ushers to seat the audience quickly, and the early completion of all preparations will insure a prompt beginning and go far toward winning the approval of the audience.

And now the first scene is ready,—in fact it has been so for several hours. The singers take their positions, and the conductor, having given a final word of encouragement and confidence takes his place down in front. The overture begins. For two hours the audience, in a spirit of generous but discriminating appreciation adventures with the people of Fairyland, with geisha girls in the cherry gardens of Japan, with Napoleon at Malmaison, or with the sailors on board His Majesty's ship, *Pinafore*.

And then come the last strains of music, the last tumult of applause. The curtain falls. The operetta is over. "Was it worth while?" the director may ask himself. "Was it worth all the time we spent in practising?" the actors may query. "Was it worth the thought and labor expended on the costumes and scenery?" the assistants may ponder. May we answer them all—"Yes, it was distinctly worth all the time and effort which you gave, individually and collectively. For when you, the director, have chosen an operetta of real merit, and when you, the performers and assistants, have given the best presentation of which you were capable, you have done that which is intensely satisfying and eminently worth while; and this you have done, not vicariously, but through your own self-expression—that avenue through which we give and receive the highest degree of enjoyment. Moreover, you have added to the sum of happiness of your own community; and hand in hand with others you have created a thing of beauty."

APPENDIX A

BIBLIOGRAPHY

On Acting

Technique of Dramatic Art—Bosworth. MacMillan, New York.
Acting—Roger and Crafton. Crofts, New York.
Problems of the Actor—Calvert. Holt, New York.
Dramatics for School and Community—Wise. Stewart Kidd Co.,
Cincinnati, Ohio.
Acting and Play Production—Andrews and Weirick. Longmans,
New York.

On Staging

Equipment for Stage Production—Krows. Appleton, New York.
Shifting Scenes of the Modern European Theatre. Coward & Mc-
Cann, New York.
The Art of the Theatre—Craig. Dodd, New York.
Secrets of Scene Painting—Van Dyke, Brown. George Routledge
and Sons, London, England.

On Lighting

Stage Lighting—Fuchs, Edison Lamp Works, Harrison, N. J.
Bulletin 146A (no charge).
The Theatre of Today—Moderwell. Dodd, New York.

On Costuming

Clothes On and Off the Stage—Chalmers. D. Appleton & Co.,
New York.
Stage Costuming—Agnes Young. MacMillan Co., New York.
Costuming the Play—Grimball and Wells. Century, New York.
Costuming and Scenery—Mackay. Henry Holt & Co., New York.
Costume and Fashion—Norris. Dutton & Co., New York.

On Dancing

The Dance and Its Place in Education—H. Doubler. Harcourt and
Brace, New York.

Dances of the People—Elizabeth Burchenal. G. Schirmer, New York.

Rhythmic Action Plays and Dances—Irene E. Phillips Moses. Milton Bradley Co., Springfield, Mass.

DYES AND DYEING (Cf. p. 11—XIV)

Dyes and Dyeing—Pellew. McBride, New York. Pamphlet—Grazalley Dye Stuff Corporation, 117 Hudson St., New York.

ON MAKE-UP

The Art of Make-up—Chalmers. D. Appleton & Co., New York.

ON THE TECHNIQUE OF GENERAL PRODUCTION

The Book of Amateur Play Production—Milton Smith. D. Appleton & Co., New York.

How to Produce Amateur Plays—Barrett Clark. Little, Brown & Co., Boston.

Community Drama—Playground and Recreation Association of America. The Century Co., New York.

A Book of Entertainment and Theatricals—Helena Smith. Dayton and Louise Bascom. Barrat-Robert, McBride & Co., N. Y.

THEATRICAL MAGAZINES

Theatre Arts Monthly—Theatre Arts, Inc., at 119 W. 57th Street, New York.

Drama Magazine, Monthly, 1008-410 S. Michigan Blvd., Chicago, Illinois.

Church and Drama, 105 East 22nd Street, New York.

APPENDIX B

THEATRICAL SUPPLY HOUSES

SCENERY AND DRAPERIES

Beaumont Scenery Studios, 443 West 47th St., New York.
I. Weiss & Sons, 508 West 43rd St., New York.
Maharam Textile Co., Inc., 107 West 48th St., New York.

STAGE LIGHTING

Pevean Color Specialty Co., 71 Brimmer St., Boston, Mass.
George L. Hall, W. Emerson Street, Melrose, Mass.

COSTUME HOUSES

CHICAGO, ILLINOIS—Fritz Schoultz, 19 West Lake.

CEDAR RAPIDS, IOWA—Wyskocil, Mrs. Mary A.

DENVER, COLORADO—Colorado Costume Company, 1751 Champa.

DES MOINES, IOWA—Wingate Company, 504 Walnut.

HOUSTON, TEXAS—Beer, Mrs. D. L., 1901½ N. Main St.
Houston Costume Co. & Hat Shop, 317½ Main St.
Stafford, Mrs. Fannie, 1139 Panama Boulevard.

KANSAS CITY, MISSOURI—Theodore Lieben, 820 Main Street.
Harralson Costume Co., 1327 Main Street.

KALAMAZOO, MICHIGAN—Ihling Bros. Everard Co., 233-239 E. Main
Street.

MEMPHIS, TENNESSEE—Memphis Costume and Regalia Co., 226 S.
Main Street.

NEW ORLEANS, LOUISIANA—Alaban, Mrs. J., 225 Bourbon.

OKLAHOMA CITY, OKLAHOMA—Empire Costume Co., 309-13 Empire Building.

OMAHA, NEBRASKA—Friedman, John, 203 Karbach.
Theo. Lieben & Son, 401 Webster—Sunderland Building.

PORTLAND, OREGON—Pan-Co Vesta Co., 182 Tenth Street.

ST. PAUL, MINNESOTA—Giesen Martin, 71 W. 4th.
Wormser Jean Costume Shop, 530 Rice.

SAN FRANCISCO, CALIFORNIA—Blake and Amber, 3d Floor, Wilson
Building, 973 Market Street.